DATE DUE

NO 4 '9			
DE 9 '94			

DEMCO 38-296

TAKING EUROPE SERIOUSLY

Taking Europe Seriously

Simon Serfaty

St. Martin's Press
New York

First published in the United States of America in 1992

Printed in the United States of America

ISBN 0-312-06231-1

Library of Congress Cataloging-in-Publication Data

Serfaty, Simon.
    Taking Europe seriously / Simon Serfaty.
        p.   cm.
    Includes bibliographical references (p.   ) and index.
    ISBN 0-312-06231-1
    1. European federation. 2. Europe 1992. I. Title.
JN15.S44 1992
321'.04'094—dc20   91-42581
                                                                           CIP

Contents

Preface

This essay was written in 1991, against the background of momentous changes in Europe and around the world. In one form or another, it returns to a number of themes presented in earlier work that dealt with the evolution of U.S. foreign policy in the Cold War, intra-European relations, and transatlantic relations. It should be read as an attempt to escape the headlines of the present in order to project into the future trends that have emerged in Europe since the end of World War II.

Shortly after he had managed the organization of the European Coal and Steel Community in 1951, Jean Monnet was asked by one of his collaborators whether Europe's agenda would next be one of "great difficulties" that would have to be used "to make further progress." "It is indeed," answered Monnet. "You've understood what Europe's all about." That was the case throughout the Cold War. It is still the case now that the Cold War is over.

This essay was much improved by Michael T. Clark, first a colleague at the Paul H. Nitze School of Advanced International Studies, and now a professor of international politics at the College of William and Mary. He read and edited the manuscript at various stages and gave valuable suggestions. I am grateful. At various stages, too, research assistance was provided by Sabine Cornelius and Susanne Rose. It was always useful and much appreciated. Finally, in preparing the essay for publication I was greatly helped by the efforts of Steve Brigham and Nancy McCoy. It is a pleasure to acknowledge them.

FOR REINETTE

1
Europe-92
in Perspective

T he subject of this book is "Europe"—an idea that has
acquired substance in a manner and to a degree scarcely
conceivable a few years ago. More specifically, "Europe" is
a community in which a small but not finite number of nation-states
in Western Europe have progressively relinquished much of their
sovereignty, and even part of their national identity, in order to
achieve an ever closer union among themselves.

Some argue that "Europe" is still a fiction because of the absence
of a broad and credible commitment to a body politic whose
supranational authority might supersede, someday, the authority of
its members. Others insist that "Europe" is already a reality, shaped
by a process that has always been politically motivated,
notwithstanding the limited economic goals that have been set and
achieved along the way. Since neither conclusion is entirely wrong,
neither can be entirely right. Both are simply exaggerated. In today's
Europe the sounds of discord continue to intrude upon the harmony
of cooperation. Yet the persistent dissonance has been overwhelmed
by an increasingly powerful refrain of unity, as the collective actions
of "Europe" now set the meter and determine the pitch in nearly
every aspect of its members' national life.

The argument presented in this book builds upon two fundamental findings. The first is that the movement toward European unity
responds to a logic that has proved, over four decades, as relentless

as it has been flexible. The logic itself is not novel in statecraft. It is simply the necessity imposed upon political communities that must choose between an increasingly diminished ability to shape alone the external conditions of their existence, and the increasingly potent opportunities unveiled by a larger, but remote, untested and unfamiliar collective entity. What is novel is that this entity has exerted its influence among communities with a sense of national identity and continuity more deeply rooted than those of almost any other political body on the planet. Yet the conditions that have brought Europe to its present juncture are not likely to disappear or become any less compelling than they have been since the end of World War II. The safest judgment, therefore, is that patterns of integration observed in Western Europe in the past will continue in the future. That such will be the case is all the more certain as the pattern exhibits an irreversible ratchet effect: no state really contemplates defection, but each step toward integration creates even more demands and needs that invariably are beyond the capacity of nation-states to manage well, if at all.

The second premise from which the argument of this book proceeds is that the external conditions that have permitted European integration to proceed as far as it has, and yet have also impeded its going further, have now begun to dissipate: namely, the conditions that made it both desirable and possible for the United States to provide its allies in Europe with the measure of military and economic security to which they became accustomed during the Cold War. As conditions in and around Europe have been radically transformed with the end of the Cold War, direct threats to American interests in and beyond Europe are less palpable than before, especially as Europe's own capacities for and interests in shaping a new order have increased dramatically. Admittedly, whether the nation-states of Europe will prove capable of speaking with a single voice, let alone acting with a single mind, is an open question. Yet the reasons for doing so are now clearer than ever.

These two developments, taken together, suggest that the time has come when the idea of Europe must be taken seriously. One of these developments shows that "Europe" is possible and draws from its recent history a method, if not yet a blueprint, for political union. The other development confirms that "Europe" is necessary and points to an emerging community of interest, if not yet of purpose. To be sure, it is not to be taken for granted that a "Europe" that is both possible and necessary must eventually come to be. But if these two premises can in fact be demonstrated, the conclusion can be escaped only on pain of tragedy.

To explain how and why Europe has been transformed, and what it has become, it is necessary to say something first about the motives and affinities of the principal actors and their supporters and rivals on and off the stage, as well as to rehearse the general movement of their collective performance. This task is briefly undertaken in the remainder of this chapter. Chapter 2 is concerned with the manner in which different states, for different reasons, have had recourse to a supranational fiction to resolve real national problems. Chapter 3 seeks to unveil the logic by which that fiction was permitted to acquire substance, while Chapter 4 inquires into the nature and quality of that substance. Finally, Chapters 5 and 6 seek to locate the new Europe in its larger setting and to outline Europe's agenda for its approaching future.

Ménage à Trois

That France has often held center stage as both the hero and the villain of this process should come as no surprise. After World War II, and throughout the forty-five years of the Cold War the constraints imposed by history on a twice-defeated Germany, and by geography on an insular Great Britain, left France, logically and inevitably, as the only nation with the capacity and will to mount a sustained drive toward European unification.[1] Thus, the grand initiatives that produced a supranational Coal and Steel Community in 1951, that sought to promote an integrated Defense Community until 1954, and that led five other states to sign the Rome Treaty in 1957 were mostly inspired by the governments of the French Fourth Republic. Three decades later, new and ambitious plans calling for economic, monetary, and even political union soon after the completion of a single market were critically, and perhaps decisively, influenced by the French Fifth Republic.

As will be shown, no one plan for and about "Europe" has ever been completed on time. As will be suggested, even under the most favorable (and least likely) circumstances of economic growth, political stability, and regional peace, delays in implementing current agreements are now even more predictable than in the past. The reason for these delays has to do with the unprecedentedly broad scope and objectives of the latest schemes.

Previously, attempts at building the European Community (EC) usually moved one step at a time: in one area only, and exclusive of the others; with one closed group of members, and without much interest in enlarging the group until the step that had been started had moved far enough toward completion. In other words, even after European institutions were launched, they had to be strengthened before they could be widened. Furthermore, after enlargement was negotiated, its consequences for the expanded Community had to be understood and accepted before any new institutional step could be taken in a direction that seemed to follow logically from the previous one. Thus, organizing a small common market took much of the decade that followed the signing of the Rome Treaty. Only in 1969 could there be any serious discussion of taking on three new members (especially with respect to Britain, but also Denmark and Ireland). But moving on to new cooperative areas (especially monetary union, which had already been discussed at the time), could not truly be enacted until the initial impact of this expansion had been absorbed ten years later.

In 1992 and beyond, however, the Community appears to be poised for a leap forward in every direction, and with any number of new members previously associated with the European Free Trade Association (EFTA) and the Council for Mutual Economic Assistance (COMECON), organizations whose establishment completed the economic and political divisions of the Cold War. There is more to this leap than the organization of a single market by December 31, 1992. Germany insists on more political union for the current twelve members and a stronger European Parliament that would give democratic legitimacy to the actions of the European Commission. France seeks monetary union, including a strong European central bank that would weaken the influence of Germany's *Bundesbank*. Spain wants more economic convergence and an end to the inequities that continue to separate the initial six members, plus Britain and Denmark, and the latest four (Greece and Portugal in addition to Ireland and Spain). Britain wants less of everything (except members, of which it claims to want more), and Italy wants more of everything (except members, about which it remains ambivalent).

However desirable such objectives may be, they all cannot be reached simultaneously, and, now as before, the timetable for "Europe" cannot be predicted with any certainty. Choices must be made. An expansion that occurred too quickly might compromise initiatives not sufficiently matured as countries that enter the Community too early would be unable to live with the discipline expected from its members. The only certainty, therefore, is that of the many failures that loom ahead: whatever the Single European Act of 1987 may say, organization of the single market will not be completed by December 31, 1992. But in no way should the predictability of failure in meeting the EC's self-imposed deadlines erode the credibility of the entire process. The history of "Europe" teaches that time can be stopped after all—that any objective not achieved on schedule, or not sought on demand, is never abandoned but only postponed.

"Europe" cannot be built all at once. Before any new beginning come many false starts. No such journey can be expected to proceed without encountering many apparent dead ends. Nor is it possible for "Europe" to be built by any one state alone. Ideally, this task should have been equally shared, and responsibility for its leadership evenly assumed, by the three dominant powers in Western Europe: Britain, France, and Germany. Clearly, the making of "Europe" would have been accelerated, and the institutions of the Community would have been strengthened, if these countries had been able to agree in any durable fashion—if, in other words, they had succeeded in overcoming their historical, cultural, and political differences and had formed a close *ménage à trois* linked to one another by a common vision of Europe's future family life. This has not been the case.

Prospects for a stable triangular relationship have emerged on occasion, of course. In October 1954 Britain's decisive role in expanding the Brussels Treaty Organization (formed with France and the Benelux countries—Belgium, the Netherlands, and Luxemburg— in 1948) into a broader Western European Union (WEU) set the stage for Germany's entry into the North Atlantic Treaty Organiza- tion (NATO) a few months later, thereby ending a major strain in Franco-German and Anglo-French relations. This apparent resolution of the two related questions of Britain's role in the European Community and Germany's status in the Atlantic community facilitated the French-sponsored Messina conference, which was held in June 1955 to relaunch "Europe" after the long and divisive intra- European and transatlantic debate over the European Defense Community. Nearly two decades later, in 1973, Britain's long- delayed entry in the Common Market also ended a contentious issue in both Anglo-French and Franco-German relations.

Britain's membership was widely expected to ease implementa- tion of the ambitious commitment to economic and monetary union made by France and Germany at The Hague in December 1969. But neither one of these moments of concord proved to be lasting, or even significant. In 1957 Britain's rejection of the Rome Treaty, which launched Europe's quest for an "ever closer union," had prevented neither Germany (because of France) nor France (because of Germany) from signing it. In 1973 a weakened Britain entered a community that was already under the influence of an increasingly cooperative Franco-German Continental couple that the insular state could neither disrupt nor reconstitute.

Over the years, all three countries have known periods of bilateral intimacy. For Britain and France, such a period came early; for France and Germany, it came later; for Britain and Germany, it has come occasionally. But because the Anglo-German courtship usually suffered from Bonn's misgivings about Britain's commit- ment to its security, Europe's two most significant couples united

France and Britain during the first decade of the postwar era (without, and even against, Germany) and, during the next three decades, France and the Federal Republic (without, and even in spite of, Britain).

In 1945 France courted Britain, the other European democracy that had won the war. French advances were doomed, however, by the mutually exclusive ambitions entertained by the two countries. In the West they competed for an extra measure of American goodwill, which would confirm their respective claims of leadership in Europe. The Anglo-Saxon logic of a special relationship between Britain and the United States prevailed over a French logic that assumed France to be anybody's preferred partner. Under Britain's watchful eye, the Fourth Republic gave priority to the Cold War and the Soviet threat so long as it hoped to become America's most trusted ally in Europe. As it became increasingly clear that no such ties could be achieved, however, French policies progressively asserted more autonomy from the United States. This reappraisal was well under way before de Gaulle's return to power in May 1958.

Failure to reverse Britain's predilection for a special relationship with the United States (and with the Commonwealth) over Europe led the French to turn to the Federal Republic, against which had been devised their earlier schemes of European unity—including the Organization for European Economic Cooperation, the European Coal and Steel Community, and the European Defense Community. Thus began a delicate *pas de deux* in Europe: the political prowess of the French ballerina, always assertive but not often gracious, came to rely on the economic strength of her German partner, always powerful but not yet domineering. The Franco-German performance was designed to parallel, or complement, a similar dance performed by the United States with Britain on the transatlantic stage.

This historic reconciliation between two countries formerly locked into centuries of hostility and war was orchestrated by Charles de Gaulle, the first president of the Fifth Republic, and Konrad Adenauer, the first chancellor of the Federal Republic. Although the intense feelings that led both countries to fear and detest each other after the war had already begun to subside by the mid-1950s, it was up to these two men, who liked, respected, and admired each other, to conceive a bilateral relationship that pledged French support for German policies in the East (namely, on unification and toward the Soviet Union) in return for German support for French policies in the West (mostly on Europe and toward Britain).[2] For added protection, de Gaulle—who was occasionally able to forgive the past but never seemed quite prepared to forget it—accelerated the development of an independent nuclear force that was designed to give his country equal status with Britain, and, not insignificantly, military superiority over the Federal Republic, which the French president expected to be permanent.

Despite moments of conflict, which were particularly sharp after Adenauer's replacement by Ludwig Erhard in October 1963, the Franco-German partnership worked generally well. Neither country could escape any longer the need to heal the psychological scars that two major wars in one generation had left on the soul of their nations and that of an entire continent. Public revolt against the horror of war had intensified as that horror had grown worse with each new war. Perhaps as a result, French and German leaders now showed an unprecedented will to work together. Differences over past events (wars), present needs (unity), and future expectations (unification) remained real and were significant. To be sure, the French would have liked the Germans to be weaker, and the Germans would have liked the French to be gentler. But no less real, and even more significant, was their shared determination to overcome or accommodate these differences. The same political will for compromise could not be found or sustained between France and Britain (although, for a brief moment in the early 1970s, President Georges Pompidou and Prime Minister Edward Heath moved toward rapprochement) or even between Britain and the Federal Republic (despite Chancellor Erhard's mistrust of France in the mid-1960s).

After "Europe" found an affluent home in the Common Market, new presidents were elected in Paris—Pompidou in 1969, Valéry Giscard d'Estaing in 1974, and François Mitterrand in 1981—at about the same pace as chancellors in Bonn—Willy Brandt in 1969, Helmut Schmidt in 1974, and Helmut Kohl in 1982. Even though no two leaders ever achieved the same degree of intimacy as de Gaulle and Adenauer, each pair left its imprint on the process of European integration. Pompidou and Brandt agreed on Britain's application for membership and took the first steps toward monetary unity and political cooperation in 1969. Schmidt and Giscard agreed on the form and structure of a European Council and organized the European Monetary System in 1978. Mitterrand and Kohl agreed on the need for revisions in the Rome Treaty and jointly managed the negotiation of the Single European Act in 1985.

The enlargement of the Community in January 1973 liberated Germany from its exclusive relationship with France. By giving Bonn the option of an occasional alignment with London, it threatened to isolate the French. Yet, in every significant instance, Britain's resistance to "Europe" ended any such threat: the resistance, that is, of Prime Minister Harold Wilson to membership, Prime Minister James Callaghan to the European Monetary System, and Prime Minister Margaret Thatcher to the Single Act—and of all three to the budgetary terms that had been negotiated by each of their predecessors. At the end of the 1980s, Kohl and Mitterrand showed, understandably, little interest in starting a *ménage à trois* with Thatcher. By then, the main obstacle was not that Britain's ideas about Europe lacked sufficient substance to influence its partners. It was, instead, that applied to a process that British leaders invariably continued to fight long after they had apparently embraced it, such ideas had lost all credibility during the four decades before Thatcher resigned from office in November 1990.

Corps de Ballet

The complex narrative of West European unification cannot be reduced to relations between Britain, France, and Germany, important as these relations have been. Also to be considered are the other member-states—the all-important *corps de ballet* that has grown in size, steadily but slowly and somewhat erratically. With countries threatening to move out, seeking to move in, or pledging to stay out, "Europe" has always evolved at different speeds. An institutional core constituted by the six original members of the European Economic Community organized by the Rome Treaty has remained one or several steps ahead of the other six countries that entered the Community—in 1973, 1981, and 1986—under economic circumstances less propitious than those that preceded and accompanied the first ten years of the Common Market. Indeed, the process of widening the membership of the EC, while deepening its institutions, has become so uneven as to make some laggard EC members less compliant with EC discipline than some non-EC members. Greece, which fought hard for membership, is now occasionally scolded by its partners because of its inability to sustain the rigor of membership; Sweden, which fought hard against membership, demonstrated its ability to accept that rigor even before its government had decided to apply for admission.

At one point or another, and usually more than once, almost every EC state, including every one of the initial Six, has played a role important enough to transform the European triangle of power into a wider circle of influence whose center was neither one of the Big Three nor even either one of the two superpowers. Italy, where the idea of Europe has always received wide public support, presents an especially compelling case among this group of Six. In the 1980s three of the most significant tests of European unity were influenced, perhaps decisively, by the Italian government: in 1983, with Prime Minister Francesco Cossiga's ability to ensure the deployment in Italy of intermediate-range nuclear forces before a vital vote in Bonn on the same question; in 1985, with Prime Minister Bettino Craxi's leadership of the Milan summit which agreed to hold the intergovernmental conference that negotiated the Single European Act; and in 1990, with Prime Minister Giulio Andreotti's presidency of the Rome summit, which agreed on an unexpectedly rapid timetable for monetary union.

Yet, because of the many limits Italy faces at home, including a well-deserved reputation for a political system that cannot effectively meet the challenging demands of its own people, let alone the demanding challenges of the Community, Italy invites serious doubt over its reliability as a co-leader of Europe. Its ministers preside over meetings of the European Council—and at the Council of Ministers, the Commission, or the Parliament—with much talent and considerable effectiveness. But the leadership they display among their European colleagues cannot be sustained over a wide variety of issues for any period of time. All too often, the pledges they make to the European Community in Brussels are ignored, diluted, or stalled by the Italian parliament in Rome, owing to the ever-present necessity of catering to the Byzantine complexities of internal party politics. As a result, Italian governments often adopt positions at home directly contrary to what they pledged to the Community, whose decisions, reached in common, are criticized or even opposed as if they had been imposed upon unwilling Italian partners. Little that happens in Brussels or in Rome ever remains what it becomes in Rome or in Brussels. No opposition is truly permanent, and, conversely, no support is truly operational. Italy's support for the Commission's single market directives may well be second to none in Brussels; however, in Rome, ratification of these directives is delayed longer than in any other EC state.

Moreover, Italy's division between a developed and affluent north, and a dependent and poor south, mirrors the divisions that exist within the Community, as well as the whole of Europe. Comparing the two parts of Italy is not unlike comparing, say, Greece to the rest of the Community. In the Mezzogiorno, per capita income amounts to less than three fifths of the national average, and the rate of unemployment is more than three times that of the north. Even as Italy's growing public debt—up from 58 percent of the gross national product in 1981 to more than 100 percent in 1990—threatens to undermine the country's ability to keep pace with European integration, its ability to rely on the Community for regional aid has been undermined by the needs of new members. Italy is now a recipient of, rather than a net contributor to, EC funds. Finally, to make matters worse, the incremental productivity gains of the 1980s, which resulted from labor shedding and the application of new technologies, have run their course. In the 1990s Italian industry is threatened with new increases in production costs that would reduce its competitiveness in the single market, and even in its own internal market, north and south.

Among the other six EC members, Britain, of course, was always a central player in the Community, because of what it did before it joined (organizing the European Free Trade Association), when it joined (threatening to break the Franco-German relationship), and even after it joined (renegotiating the terms to which it had just agreed). But outside of Britain, Spain is probably the country most likely to near co-leadership status in the future.

As has been the case with other late applicants, Spain's EC membership did not come easily. At first Spain was denied admission in the European Community, as well as in the Atlantic community, on grounds of democratic felony. In France, especially, memories of General Franco's ties with nazi Germany and fascist Italy caused much opposition to entertaining a formal request for admission. Even after Franco's death, however, the many years of bitter arguments that followed Spain's application (considered jointly with that of Portugal) confirmed that EC membership is not debated only over political questions of democratic governance.

With Europe still in the midst of an EC-wide economic recession, the budgetary cost of taking on two new members, both poor, was deemed prohibitive as the first bills on Greece's membership, in 1981, were about to be presented to the Community for payment. Moreover, the Community was itself facing political stagnation, in part caused by its inability to settle the various issues surrounding the first round of EC enlargement, from six to nine members. Late in 1982 economic recovery in the United States provided the Community with the locomotive needed for political recovery, as it coincided with the first indications that the 1979 European Monetary System might work after all. Membership could be granted, then, to both Spain and Portugal at the Fontainebleau summit in 1984. At the time, Spain's socialist leader, Felipe González, enjoyed close relations with other socialist leaders in the EC—especially François Mitterrand and Bettino Craxi. And, as had also been the case with Britain's application, ending the debate over membership was viewed by all members, including France and Germany, as a political prerequisite to moving on with Europe's ambitious agenda for an institutional relaunching of the Community.

Yet, unlike Britain, whose reputation for opposing "Europe" often denies its government the influence to which it is entitled by history, Spain, through its support for "Europe," has gained an influence that is in excess of its resources. Four decades of authoritarian leadership left the country and its government well prepared to abandon a piece of national sovereignty that seemed of diminished significance in order to gain a share of regional identity that appeared of growing importance. Politically, Spain joined France and Italy, but also Portugal and Greece, into an EC grouping of southern states that might act as a counterweight to the more conservative states in northern Europe and that could protect the EC's Mediterranean vocation in the Middle East and North Africa. Economically, Spain's swelling demographic curve, the availability of cheap labor, and a solid network of communications make it one of the more attractive national markets in Europe, one that attracts non-EC firms wishing to strengthen their presence in, or gain access to, the Community. Within the Community, the Spanish prime minister's status as the youngest elder statesman of Europe has helped Felipe González emerge as the possible heir of an earlier generation of European statesmen mostly issued from the small northern countries of Belgium and Holland. For many of these reasons, no other country in Europe can make its experience after 1975 as distinctly relevant to the experience of much of Eastern Europe since 1989.

Pas de Deux

Throughout the Cold War, Europe's choreography was directed by the two countries that had truly won the war against Germany: the United States, whose status as an extra-European power gave it a role that threatened, once more, to be essentially offstage, and the Soviet Union, whose presence on the Continent kept it, more than ever before, center stage. Each superpower expected the other to bring its troops home quickly after the war: one, located on the

European continent, because it was too weak to stay, and the other, located on another continent, because it was too strong to care. Yet, with suspicion from and about one side breeding ever more suspicion about and from the other, the two countries soon started a process of competitive force deployment on both sides of Europe, each in its own way but arguably because of the other.

Thus emerged the postwar status quo in a continent that was neither whole nor freed from the domination or ambitions of totalitarian power. In the West, U.S. leadership was accepted to resist Soviet-inspired subversion or worse (and also to deny another explosion of German power). In the East, Soviet control was imposed to deny U.S.-inspired intrusion or worse (whether directly or through one of the USSR's proxies, especially Germany). The resulting stalemate left each superpower with the semblance of success over its rival. That no territorial change in Europe occurred after the 1948 coup in Czechoslovakia was an American victory against the Soviet threat—given all the reality it needed by the pervasiveness of Soviet ideology and the brutality of Soviet power. That there could be no rollback of the Soviet gains achieved in the East before the Czech coup was a Soviet victory against the American threat—given some of the reality it needed by the renewed vigor of a German-led European Economic Community and the strength of a U.S.-led Atlantic Alliance.

At first, the Soviet Union was a more credible European power than the United States. This was not a matter of geography alone. The United States built itself as a nation in opposition to the nations of Europe and its divisions. It defined its relations with its neighbors in the Western Hemisphere, and elsewhere in the world, in isolation from, and even against, Europe and its ways. In 1919 the United States began its life as a great power with a renewed demonstration of its national commitment to being left alone. In 1945 the experience of World War II did not suffice to reverse these historical preferences and transform the United States into a European power—a power, that is, whose interests in Europe would have been so vital as to make life without Europe difficult to contemplate, let alone endure.

On the contrary, it was the interest that the Europeans had in preserving America's interest in their fate that shaped the U.S. commitment to, and presence in, Europe. In 1949 the North Atlantic Treaty was signed mostly because the countries of Europe wanted it. Even if they did not always seem to agree against whom the treaty was organized, they surely understood why they needed it. "Europe," on the other hand, took its first steps toward unity mostly because the United States sought it. Even if American statesmen did not always seem to understand how (that is, with whom) it would be built, they surely perceived the need for ending the fragmentation of the past. In both cases allies and community members were all the more enthusiastic as, apparently, everyone was pleased and no one was hurt. By 1949 the Soviet Union could no longer be considered an ally, but it was still too early to fear it as the unambiguously dangerous and implacable adversary it became only later in the Cold War. Similarly, Germany could no longer be viewed as an adversary, but it was still too early to cultivate it as the stable and reliable ally it became only in later years.

America's rise as a European power resulted from the Cold War and was a direct consequence of the rise of Soviet power in Europe. Yet, even after the outbreak of the Cold War, U.S. objectives remained relatively limited. Without an explicit American decision to launch an offensive war aimed at the liberation of Eastern Europe, the Continent's divisions could be ended only by the superpower that had used force to impose its presence outside its own borders. Accordingly, for more than four decades, the Soviet Union policed the boundaries of the status quo in Europe. Not even the periods of détente that followed Stalin's death in 1953 and the Cuban missile crisis in 1962, and that accompanied the final phase of the Vietnam War beginning in 1972, ever gave rise to hopes of ending the postwar divisions of Europe—a continent irreversibly split between two military alliances (and a few neutral states), responsive to two dominant ideologies (and some ambiguous political shades), and divided by many national boundaries (and even more nationalities inside and across them).

If anything, the prospects for change that occasionally emerged were received with even more apprehension, as it was feared that any real change could only come from the East at the expense of the West. After Vietnam, America grew impatient with the demands placed by its European allies on its dwindling resources. After Watergate, Europe lost its confidence in American leadership, which appeared to display some of the worst political features that had characterized its own governments. After détente, the Soviet Union relied on the military parity enshrined in the first Strategic Arms Limitation Talks (SALT) agreement to assert its new ambitions in the Third World. Thus, at the end of the 1970s, the future of America's relations with Western Europe faced the combined scourges of Eurocommunism, which undermined the desirability of any sort of U.S.-European ties, Europessimism, which questioned the feasibility of European unity, and American decline, which threatened the credibility of the American protection.

That the depth of Western decline, as compared with the height of Soviet ascendancy, was grossly exaggerated is all too obvious. In the late 1980s it was the Soviet Union that became indifferent to the fate of its empire abroad as it uncovered the overwhelming evidence of its domestic failure. After the Soviet Union had revealed surprising passivity toward the fact and the pace of anticommunist revolutions in Eastern Europe in 1989, Moscow's acquiescence to Germany's unification on Western terms in 1990, as well as its indifference to its former clients in the Third World in 1991, confirmed a formerly unthinkable prospect: that of a weak and divided Russia anxious to be given some living space in the common house of a strong and uniting Western Europe.

Entr'acte

In 1990 the Cold War ended, therefore, with two overlapping but distinct processes of change in Europe intimately influenced by the *pas de deux* that the two superpowers had staged throughout the previous decades. Understood as a direct challenge to the primacy of the nation-state that has been under way for more than forty years, change in Western Europe is less the triumph of American power than of American values. The often predicted but never expected revolutions of Eastern Europe were made possible by the collapse of the Soviet leadership's will to use its power to preserve an empire acquired by force: they represent a total defeat for Soviet ideas of governance far more than a defeat of Soviet power. In effect, the states of Western Europe are well on their way toward what the Truman administration hoped they would become after World War II, and what the countries of Eastern Europe now hope to become after the Cold War: democratic, stable, affluent, and united.

Nevertheless, because neither of these processes will be completed before many more years, they both leave the European continent in the throes of competing transitions whose final outcomes can still be affected by the lingering shadow of a Soviet military power that has been crippled politically but not defeated on the field. In Western Europe the EC states still hesitate before the leap forward contemplated for 1992 and beyond: they stand at a crossroad between the promise of more integration in ever more significant sectors and the threat of new setbacks with ill-defined consequences. In Eastern Europe the euphoria of liberation fades, sobered by the dangers of a prewar legacy of regional conflicts and internal divisions, neglected but not resolved during the Cold War. Standing with one territorial foot on each side of the Continent is Germany. Unified at last, it is not yet united, torn between a dominant West that wallows in its affluence and a subservient East that resents its continued squalor. And woven into each part of the Continent, the United States and the Soviet Union are joined belatedly into a sudden and wholly unexpected embrace while still having to attend to the preservation of their legitimate interests within the new scheme that will result from the uneven end of their respective hegemonies in Europe.

If there were no threats left to deter, there would be little point about arguing over the most effective ways of containing and controlling danger. Because none of the processes of change in Europe have been completed, however, parts of the status quo inherited from the past are still needed, at least for a while. However much relevance they have lost, the postwar structures are unlikely to be allowed to disappear in the absence of any new structures. What will these new structures be, under whose auspices will they emerge, with and against whom will they be sustained? Responding to these questions in the immediate aftermath of the Cold War remains as premature as it was, say, in 1947, shortly after the end of World War II. But it is hardly too early to be reminded, in the name of prudence, how self-defeating is the temptation to take security for granted.

Fears of a future that is neither known nor fully predictable grow out of a past that is known well, even if it is not always clearly understood. Divisions in Europe long preceded the Cold War and its related military and ideological rivalries. In fact, obviously short-lived, these conflicts were minor, compared with centuries of deeply rooted institutional anarchy throughout the European continent. Said, heard, and viewed together, the *déjà dit* about a fading North Atlantic Treaty Organization, the *déjà entendu* about a strengthened European Community and a reborn Western European Union, and the *jamais vu* of a European political community and the Conference on Security and Cooperation in Europe (CSCE) anticipate, but do not create, a new security architecture.

In 1991, events in the Gulf, in the Baltic states and in most other Soviet republics, and in Yugoslavia as well as elsewhere in Eastern Europe have confirmed further that none of these institutions can change too quickly, none too slowly. If NATO were to be abandoned suddenly and U.S. forces withdrawn precipitously, if the institutional growth of the Community were to be postponed indefinitely and its expansion stalled for too long, if dependence on such vague and ill-defined institutions as the WEU or CSCE were to be asserted prematurely, the end of the Cold War, which is irreversible, might give way to intra-national instabilities and international conflicts whose history in Europe, far from being ended, is just now being revived.

The irony is there for everyone to see. During the Cold War, risks of instability in Eastern and central Europe existed, of course. Many a war game began around a domestic upheaval imagined, all too realistically, in Poland or in one of its neighbors. The risks, then, had to do with Soviet intervention—a perspective that often invited Western planners to passivity and indifference. Since the end of the Cold War, risks of Soviet intervention have faded. Passivity and indifference are now the favored options of Soviet planners. What is feared instead is the necessity of Western intervention—a perspective that is inviting planners everywhere to launch a difficult reappraisal of each state's and each institution's role in Europe.

A new architecture limited to the Western pillars provided by NATO and the EC would leave little place for the Soviet Union and its former allies in central and Eastern Europe. With formal expansion to the East likely to take place neither in the Atlantic Alliance (because of the unwillingness of its members to extend its guarantee of security to their former adversaries) nor in the Community (at least for the balance of this century, and probably many years into the next), a vehicle most commonly identified for the return of these countries into Europe is the Conference on Security and Cooperation in Europe. It should be all too clear, however, that the conditions that might prompt the emergence of the CSCE as a central pillar of a new security system for Europe are not yet met. As a security neutral organization, opened to all and requiring approval from all, it would be no more effective than the League of Nations during the interwar period. At best, the CSCE will prove the ultimate umbrella for a Europe that is "whole and free" only after this lofty goal has been fulfilled by other means—that is, after there is no longer any security threat to be met through the Atlantic Alliance, after there are no longer any economic inequities that can be alleviated within the European Community, and even after there are no longer any political incompatibilities that can be moderated in the Council of Europe.

To be sure, these venues—Atlantic with the United States, *communautaire* with the nation-state, and European with the USSR—are neither separate nor mutually exclusive. Much of the interest in an architectural device that would go beyond NATO and the EC and its related parts has to do with the perceived need to accommodate the Soviet Union's and its republics' pleas for inclusion in the West. As Mikhail Gorbachev argues that neither side lost the Cold War, he conveniently suggests that both sides won and that the Soviets are entitled, therefore, to sharing the rewards of victory with the United States in some form of economic and political Grand Bargain.

But the Soviets lost, of course. Their leaders failed in their ambitions to dominate Western Europe. Their ideology failed in its attempt to subvert the West and gain a permanent foothold in the East. And their party failed in its goal to create a new society at home. The West won. Its leaders succeeded in achieving the goals of containment, rollback, and integration. Its ideology—including democracy and free enterprise—succeeded in taking root throughout Europe and beyond. And its polities succeeded in creating new societies at home. For the United States, specifically, the price of victory was high—higher than the post-World War II visionaries ever imagined. Paradoxically enough, the rewards of victory will prove to be equally high and tangible only if the potential consequences of the Soviet loss are contained. Thus, addressing the Soviet question is not a matter of Soviet right but one of Western interest, which the new architecture of Europe, built around the Atlantic Alliance and the European Community, must take into account even if it need not integrate its former adversaries in its midst, or at least not yet.

Since the Cold War the paradox of Atlantic relations is that a stronger and uniting European Community is needed if a strong and united America is to remain in Europe. Taking "Europe" seriously, in and beyond 1992, need not be done, therefore, at the expense of the victorious superpower's interests and influence. With the European Community, some find it difficult to take seriously the future of America as a European power. But without the Atlantic community, it may prove even more difficult to take seriously the future of "Europe." Each community was designed to complement the other: one deterred the threat of aggression from without, the other ended the threat of aggression from within. There can be no divorce. In the continental space dominated by the European Community, there continues to be plenty of room for the United States. In the Atlantic space dominated by the United States, there must be room for a strong and united "Europe."

2
Remembering Europe During the Cold War

I n 1945 Britain had confirmed its rank as a great power, France seemed poised to regain it, and Germany had lost it. Or, at least, this is the way each country envisioned its postwar future. Accordingly, Britain saw itself as the equal of the United States and the Soviet Union, France thought of itself as a third force between them, and Germany was mostly viewed as their future battlefield. From every vantage, a united Europe was hailed as the most suitable vehicle for a quick recovery from the war and for a final escape from future wars on the Continent. Both Britain and France expected to lead such a new Europe, with or without the other, and with the United States, though not necessarily against the Soviet Union. Defeated, divided, and disarmed, Germany wanted to be brought back into the community of European states by any of the Western countries that had defeated Hitler, but against none of them.

In Europe, Britain expected privileged treatment from the United States, as the pro-Soviet outlook of a strong and assertive communist party undermined whatever remained of French credibility in Washington. France, however, also expected U.S. support, because of Britain's resistance to the kind of supranational Europe that the Truman administration envisioned and that the French government pretended to endorse. Finally, Germany, too, expected substantial benefits from a close relationship with the United States, if only because leaving its territory at the mercy of its neighbors would add to the instability of a continent already exposed to a growing threat from the Soviet Union.

At the beginning of the Cold War the missing ingredient in the West was not, therefore, the willingness of Britain, France, or Germany to cooperate with the United States but the inability of these states to cooperate with one another. Yet the lack of effective intra-European cooperation damaged transatlantic relations. Without a sustained *ménage à trois* in Europe, the *pas de deux* performed by any two of these three countries—especially France with Britain at first, but also France and the Federal Republic of Germany in subsequent years—invariably clashed with the *pas de deux* staged by the United States with any one of them—especially Britain at first, and Germany later.

Europa, Europa

After World War II, the idea of Europe developed about and around Germany. In a postwar context not yet dominated by the emerging bipolar confrontation between the United States and the Soviet Union, European unity was acknowledged as a necessity imposed upon nation-states by their inability to attend, alone, to the threat that had already caused two major wars in thirty years. That threat was not the Soviet Union, at least not yet, but Germany. Defeated but not disabled, divided but not dissected, Germany retained an unsettling dynamism. Placing its power at the disposal of a fiction called "Europe" would deflect and harness its potent energy and remove Germany's recurring temptation to force a divided Europe into a new reich. This vision of Europe was, therefore, the continuation of the most traditional forms of *realpolitik* by other means. Both Britain and France pretended to speak in the name of Europe in order to reclaim the historical influence that, as London and Paris both feared, had been seriously weakened by the war. But where Britain spoke of a European security architecture that would be built with Germany, eventually unified, France aimed at an architecture that would keep its historical enemy permanently divided.

Jean Monnet's vision, although closer to the French view than the British view of the German problem, leapt one large step beyond established French (and European) policy. Countervailing force exerted by one state through traditional alliances with others had failed to avoid war. The European system itself had to be transformed, and the German no less than the French national identity recast within a new mold. A retroactive peace based upon punishment for past conduct was not a solution. Only persuasion, exerted by the many through the process of regional integration, could now succeed in preserving peace. "We failed in 1919 because we introduced discrimination," Monnet warned French Foreign Minister Robert Schuman late in the decade. "Peace," he added, "can be founded only on equality of rights." Contemptuous of intergovernmental cooperation, Monnet vaguely anticipated a European federation, which he hoped to base on an Anglo-French union (returning to one of Churchill's wartime proposals). But such a union was not to be. In 1949 Monnet's proposal for a merger of the French and British economies was flatly dismissed in both capitals.[1]

Fears of being isolated with Germany in Europe were especially evident in France, even though, at war's end, the harsh tone of the French discourse on Germany's future was not substantively different from that of most other members of the Grand Alliance: many Germanys (that is, more than one) would make Europe safer. Even after Germany's territory had been amputated—with Poland's extension into East Germany, but also with the disposition of the Rhineland, the Ruhr, and the Saar—the country was, therefore, to be divided into several zones of occupation with truncated sovereignty. But this objective demanded Soviet support to help balance the more benign attitude shown in Britain and, more significantly, in the United States. Hence the Franco-Soviet pact of December 1944, which pledged immediate aid or assistance against any "new German aggression or any action that might render possible a new act of aggression."[2] That Stalin dismissed the marginal contribution of

France to the war, as he did at Yalta a few weeks later, was of little consequence to the French. What they needed was not a demonstration of Soviet goodwill toward them but reassurances about the availability of Soviet power against Germany. Goodwill came from Churchill, at whose insistence a French zone of occupation in Germany was carved out of the American and British zones.[3]

These measures could not provide sufficient security for Europe, however. Even as the French imagined Stalin as the ultimate obstacle to Germany's resurgence, they feared also that, in the absence of any countervailing power from a divided Germany and a weakened France, Soviet ascendancy would end any pretense of a balance on the Continent. United into a Grand Alliance, the Western Christians had been joined by the Soviet Commissar to defeat the German Cannibal. When the Commissar in Moscow continued to starve the Cannibals in Germany, now the beneficiaries of misplaced Western charity, the French were not displeased. Had it not been for the need to abide by the American leadership, they would have been delighted to join Moscow in its systematic dismantlement of the German economy.

But the Soviet Union also required containment. France hoped to reinsure the security structure it sought with Moscow on the European continent with unprecedented guarantees from the two Anglo-Saxon islands in the West. With neither of the principal allies willing to give the French much credit for helping win the war, they were relying on their diplomatic agility to seize the initiative in winning the peace that had eluded them in 1919. The Anglo-French treaty, signed symbolically at Dunkirk in 1947, paralleled the agreement signed by Stalin and de Gaulle earlier. And, better yet, so did the North Atlantic Treaty that was signed with the United States and ten other countries in 1949. The former provided reassurances in the event of the future development of German power; the latter provided reassurances in the event of future expansion of Soviet power. That these commitments might impose severe constraints on French freedom of maneuver was obvious. Thought of independent action had already become a distant memory.

For France, the future, about to be captured by the Cold War (and dominated by the Soviet threat), was pitted against the past, embodied in World War II (and remembered as the German threat). In ways that seemed strange and contradictory to the United States, the Fourth Republic assumed complementarity between its alliances with Moscow, London, and Washington. Germany remained the principal enemy, of course: given such a formidable foe, France welcomed any other state as a friend. For different reasons in each case, no one state could be trusted fully by a nation whose rank and role in Europe could only be evoked in the past tense. As one of France's better known moralists had put it, much earlier and in a different context, "France, no longer feeling herself mistress of her situation, was beginning to shriek with terror, like a blind man without its stick or an infant that had lost its nurse."[4] By similar measures France had been failed twice, in 1914 and 1939. Now, its people shrieked with terror, many of them by rallying to various brands of isms; now, its government looked for new methods and new measures.

With a stick called Europe, France claimed to hold to a vision; with a nurse called America, France hoped it would soon regain its health. Aimed at the dual threat of German revival and Soviet expansion, early French designs for European unity were explicitly placed within a context that included Europe with Britain, and America with Europe. Initially, these preferences appeared to be shared by London. Earlier than any other postwar political leader, Winston Churchill based his support for European unity, with France at its center, on his anticipation of the conflict with the Soviet Union. Like Stalin, too, he viewed "a strong, independent, and friendly France" as a central feature of the postwar balance in Europe.[5] Without Britain, continental Europe would be left to Soviet dominance, since there would be no option to seeking the sort of diplomatic approach made with the Franco-Soviet pact. Like most other European leaders, however, Churchill also viewed European unity as a protective device against the unreliability of U.S. leadership. Europe, therefore, would permit Britain to escape exclusive dependence on the United States for its own security and that of its empire.

The advent of the Cold War removed many of the ambiguities in early postwar Anglo-French and transatlantic relations. For all the allies, the European idea and the Atlantic idea became the complementary features of a security structure designed to keep Germany in, the United States with, and the Soviet Union out of Western Europe. But the task of building European unity in such a way as to preserve the Anglo-American guarantees gained after the war remained primarily a matter of French concern. After the demise of the European Defense Community in August 1954, French policy still aimed at strengthening America's commitment to Europe. After the collapse of the joint Anglo-French intervention at Suez in November 1956, it still expected that Britain's membership in the European Economic Community (EEC) about to be launched by the Rome Treaty would consolidate Britain's presence in Europe.

Britain's decision to stay out of the EEC resulted in part from an unstated assumption that the it was unlikely to work and in part from a belief that association "with" Europe could bring all the economic benefits associated with the Common Market without entailing the political costs of membership "in" Europe. But after the many refusals issued from London to previous calls for unity, even, and especially, the most committed Europeanists had concluded that "Europe" could no longer wait for Britain. "My mind has been made up, my attitude clear," had complained a visibly exasperated Paul-Henry Spaak, a leading proponent of European unity, when he announced his resignation from the presidency of the Council of Europe. "I do not say to you: 'Let's build Europe, taking our lead from Britain,' for to rely on Britain, whether Conservative or Labor, means in the present situation, to give up the very idea of building Europe."[6] Spaak was not wrong, and his admonishment was not ignored. Over the years, Britain's opposition remained consistent. In time, however, its Continental partners came to recognize that Britain's subsequent reversal was as inevitable as its initial opposition was predictable.

Not surprisingly, French ideas for Europe were viewed suspiciously in Germany as a galling attempt to make its division permanent and its loss of sovereignty irreversible. These suspicions had a strong basis in fact, even after the merger of the three Western zones of occupation had become all but certain. In 1948, for example, French insistence on denying Germany official representation in the meetings of the Organization for European Economic Cooperation (OEEC) were seen as a naked attempt to reduce the German share of Marshall Plan aid. Already, the French claimed, Germany was receiving more assistance than it deserved, or even required; its economy, which had been disabled rather than ruined during the last months of the war, was recovering more quickly than the other economies of Western Europe.[7] French logic—why help rebuild a German economy that had been scheduled for dismantlement in the name of security against Germany's national power?—clashed with American pragmatism—why dismantle now what would have to be rebuilt later in the name of security against Soviet power?

The reality of the security problem posed by Germany for France and others in Europe was readily acknowledged by Konrad Adenauer, whose impeccable wartime credentials had quickly carried him to the leadership of the Christian Democratic Union. In contrast with Kurt Schumacher, his counterpart in the Social Democratic Party, Adenauer welcomed the primacy of foreign policy at this particular juncture in German history. Therefore, and again in contrast with Schumacher, he was willing to place the goal of Germany's unification at the bottom of his priorities, where his Western allies wanted it to be. As reward for his compliance, Adenauer expected to gain the concessions that would end the many postwar restrictions imposed on German sovereignty, thereby returning at least one half of the nation to a status that could not yet, and might never, be claimed by the other half.

That West Germany would take a seat in the Ruhr Authority, even though the Authority was empowered to make decisions on prices, quotas, and transport arrangements for German coal, coke, and steel; that it would become an associate member of the Council of Europe, even though the Council's invitation to the Saar implied the region's formal separation from Germany; that it would partici-pate in the small Europe envisioned by the European Coal and Steel Community (ECSC), even though the Community's political aim was all too obvious: these were all decisions that went against Schumacher's own preferences. In response, however, the Western allies reduced substantially the degree and scope of reparations, returned responsibility for decartelization to the German government, increased the size of ships permitted to be built in Germany, allowed the opening of German consulates abroad, welcomed Germany's OEEC representatives in Paris, and so forth. Coming only four years after the end of a war whose atrocities had set new standards, and about which Germany's responsibility was not questioned, least of all by Schumacher, these concessions, all formally written in the agreements that brought the Federal Republic of Germany into being in 1949, showed that Adenauer's flexibility had opened the door for numerous rewards.

Nor were Adenauer's policies aimed only at recovering his country's national sovereignty. Also at issue were questions of security, especially against the Soviet Union. If Germany remained disarmed, how would security be provided and at what cost to its sovereignty? If it remained divided, how would its sovereignty be restored and at what cost to its security? If it agreed to rearm, what retaliatory measures would follow from its adversaries? If it refused, what compensatory steps would be taken by its allies? Negotiating with the Soviet Union might lead to early unification, but on terms (disarmament and neutrality) that denied both sovereignty and security. Joining the emerging Atlantic and European communities of the West would sharpen the hostility of the East (at the expense of unification, at least for a time), but it would also provide a real measure of security and sovereignty.

Adenauer's willingness to cooperate with the occupying powers did not satisfy Schumacher, however. For him, Germany's future in and with Europe, with or against the United States, was to be debated in terms of an uncompromising commitment to unification.[8] Germany's entry in the North Atlantic Treaty Organization, and its participation in the European Defense Community, warned Schumacher, would lock the Federal Republic in a narrow political box *à la française* that presupposed the absence of any other Germany, and in a broader military alliance *à l'américaine* that postulated the willing sacrifice of both Germanys. The price of such political designs and military plans was that any prospect of unification would have to be abandoned, possibly permanently, without further achieving either security or even stability for Germany's Western half. In Schumacher's view, Adenauer's "collaboration with the occupation" was predicated on making Germany's territory hostage to both East and West, and, in the event of conflict, the battlefield of conquest as well as the battlefield of liberation. Such a policy, he argued, condemned a divided German people to becoming the main casualties of a two-way scorched-earth policy imposed upon them by the armies of the East and of the West waging battle for the half of the continent they did not yet control.[9]

In the Federal Republic the moral and aesthetic example set by Schumacher in resisting Hitler gave him an authority that was matched by few other German political leaders at the time, including Adenauer, and left him with an unchallenged grip on his party until his death in August 1953. Outside the Federal Republic, however, the bitter edge of Schumacher's personality, the aggressive tone of his rhetoric, and his uncompromising, relentless emphasis on Germany's unification aggravated Western anxieties. Compared with Schumacher, whose leadership Dean Acheson opposed as "harsh and violent" and whose ideas he criticized as "nationalist and aggressive," Konrad Adenauer presented an easy choice as "our" man in Bonn. According to Acheson, only the Christian Democratic Union collectively, and its leader personally (whose election as the Federal Republic's first chancellor was decided by his own vote in the German *Bundestag* in 1949), "could travel the road along which all our measures for the recovery and security of Europe had been moving." As for the Social Democratic Party, it would first need to be "relieved" of Schumacher's leadership before it could "resume a constructive role in German political life."[10]

As events confirmed in later years, Acheson was right, although probably for the wrong reasons. Neither Schumacher nor his successor, Erich Ollenhauer, accepted the refusal of every power in and out of Europe to support German demands for unification. In the West the kind of unified Germany envisaged by the social democrats was feared as a weak and neutral state that would accommodate Soviet demands, or, conversely, as a strong and domineering independent state that might become oblivious to Western influence. In the East the kind of unified Germany envisaged by Adenauer and the christian democrats was feared as a strong revanchiste state that could act just as easily alone or in alliance with the countries of the West. On both sides of the Iron Curtain, therefore, division was preferred to unification, notwithstanding the disingenuous four-power negotiations designed to strengthen the status quo while pretending to seek change. In the West the status quo was more attractive than the Soviet offer of a reunited, but disarmed and neutral, Germany; in the East the status quo was preferable to the American proposal for a reunited, but rearmed and aligned, Germany.

In any case, after Germany's entry in NATO and the establishment of the Warsaw Pact in May 1955, little room was left for compromise. With the two German governments now entrenched in two hostile military blocs, reunification was no longer an issue. This being the case, the social democrats no longer had a viable foreign policy, whether toward an alliance with the United States in NATO or toward an alliance with France in the European Community. Indeed, many of the early opponents of rearmament—including a young Willy Brandt and an even younger Helmut Schmidt—lost no time in becoming the most determined supporters of the *Bundeswehr* and NATO. But given the growing prosperity achieved by the policies of the Christian Democratic Union—Ludwig Erhard's so-called economic miracle—the social democrats no longer had an electorally viable economic policy either. The stage was then set for the party's agonizing reappraisal, at Bad Godesberg in November 1959, which Acheson had anticipated would be required to restore the party's political legitimacy in the Federal Republic and among its allies.

Thus, what closed Germany's internal debate over reunification (and, accordingly, over membership in both NATO and the European Community) were, first, the threats of insecurity from without and, second, the promises of affluence from within. Absent credible expressions of Soviet good intentions—namely, a removal of all tangible threats of aggression from without or subversion from within—a dual Atlantic and European identity was indispensable for Germany's political legitimacy, economic recovery, and military security. Thenceforth, the Federal Republic would be committed to remaining a good and reliable partner for both the United States in NATO and France in Europe, a decision that served German objectives well, including the objective of unification, as was seen three decades later.

Atlantis Resisted

Whether or not a united Europe would be a reliable partner of the United States remained a moot question for many years. After 1945, the United States provided consistent support for European unity, even at some cost to its own economic interests, and the path of cooperative efforts on the Continent paralleled that of America's rise as a European power. As the Atlantic Alliance was conceived, the OEEC gathered the beneficiaries of the Marshall Plan. As NATO was born, the Council of Europe took in all the countries that escaped Soviet control, and the ECSC brought the Federal Republic into this first supranational European Community. As the Atlantic community was about to be enlarged and strengthened, the Western European Union was organized after the European Defense Community had been defeated. In the mid-1950s new steps toward a European Economic Community were also defined in terms of the United States: catching up with the senior partner that had provided both affluence and security demanded that the American model of economic affluence and political governance be adopted, or at least duplicated as closely as possible, on the Continent.

From the start, the EEC was more than an attempt to form a European market conducive to the economies of scale achieved in the United States. On sheer economic grounds the French, especially, did not like the idea at all, which went against the state's tradition of protecting the nation's economy. This reluctance was overcome only after the Suez debacle demonstrated the political necessity of building a Europe that might eventually achieve, selectively, an autonomy of action for the defense of interests and priorities not shared by the United States.[11] To this extent the Rome Treaty was also envisioned as a preliminary step toward ending Europe's exclusive dependence on U.S. tutelage.

Coming at a time when the Cold War was about to enter one of its most difficult phases, and perhaps its most dangerous one (from the Soviet intervention in Hungary in 1956 to the Cuban missile crisis in 1962), this exercise in collective self-delusion grew logically out of the ambivalence shown by the states of Western Europe toward U.S. leadership since the end of the war. If nothing else, the humiliation of defeat shared by most countries in Europe, and their subsequent reliance on outside benefactors, sharpened an attitude whose bitterness, voiced in all European capitals, predictably caused resentment on the other side of the Atlantic. The New World might well have become indispensable to the recovery and security of the Old, but Europe still thought well enough of its worldly experience to find its contribution indispensable to the exercise of America's leadership. This had been deemed true of Roosevelt during the war. "I proceed by suggestion in order to influence matters in the right direction," Churchill reportedly told de Gaulle about his relationship with the U.S. president. The practice was continued with Truman after the war.[12]

In effect, Europeans looked upon the rise of an admittedly muscular but allegedly uncultured America through the same lenses Greeks had viewed the rise of Rome in an earlier age. The self-induced decline they faced was attributed to some obscure malaise, whose source was traced to an imported plague they labeled "Americanization." As they viewed the rise of a self-assured and dominant superpower on the other side of the Atlantic, whose institutions they were prepared to adopt as a model, the Europeans imagined a mythical America, whose intellectual flaws they were especially anxious to exaggerate so long as they remained unable to match its material strengths. So busy were they denouncing the imbalance between American power and American wisdom that they neglected to reconcile their own national and regional ambitions with their palpable weaknesses. So anxious were they to deprecate their senior partner's political experience and condemn its imperial proclivities that they overlooked their own bloody experience and brutal empires. So convinced were they that they could resume their role in the world by gaining further influence over U.S. policies that they neglected to devise policies they could truly call their own.

With or without the benefit of hindsight, it remains difficult to comprehend how so many Europeans, most of them generally well-disposed toward Americans, could have persistently entertained such distorted and frequently absurd notions. Leaving aside doubts over motives and objectives, which often prevailed on the political Left, U.S. policies were condemned simultaneously as too rigid and too inconsistent. In other words, even as Europeans felt threatened by the manner in which the United States might attend to the defense of the West, they feared, too, that such defense might not be sustained long enough. Thus the long-term credibility of the U.S. postwar commitment to the security of Europe was a constant irritant during the earliest phase of the Cold War. If this commitment was to last no longer than the time needed to recreate an indigenous balance of power on the Continent, then the major European powers needed to make sure that such a balance could outlive the end of the American involvement.

But even apart from recurring doubts that the American commitment would be sustained over time, which it obviously was, there were also widespread apprehensions about its desirability. Isolated for too long from the maelstrom of European politics, and imbued too deeply with sentiments that had little to do with the realities of world politics, American diplomats were said to be ill prepared for the management of a European balance that could not be reduced to the containment of the Soviet threat alone and that could not be defeated with a military strategy only. And, even more pointedly, the allies also anticipated an incompatibility of transatlantic interests between European countries that would find it difficult to live without their empires in the Third World (as their senior partner would have liked) and an American hegemon that would find it even more difficult to live with an empire of its own (which, its junior partners assumed, would inevitably form).

Skepticism about America's leadership was reinforced by the doubts Americans themselves had about accepting the role that two wars in Europe had imposed upon them. This is not the place to return to a debate, now largely settled, over who (if anyone) or what (if anything) caused the Cold War. Suffice it to say that reluctance in the United States to assume indefinitely the chore of guaranteeing Europe's security was no less real in 1945 than it had been in 1919. On occasion, that reluctance would be expressed in a tone, designed to bring foes and allies alike into a quick submission to the American voice of reason, that could only be offensive to all. Truman often appeared to have less patience with enemies abroad than with adversaries in Congress: by the time of his first meetings with Soviet Foreign Minister Molotov on April 22-23, 1945, he had already decided "to lay it on the line" with his interlocutor; by the time of the first postwar conference at Potsdam three months later, he had already concluded that "force is the only thing that the Russians understand."[13] As they witnessed this display of assertiveness, European diplomats showed a mixture of envy and resentment, anger and condescension. They urged their American counterparts to think, supposedly more realistically, along the lines of European ideas—even as, less convincingly, the Europeans sometimes behaved as though they had control over the panoply of American power.

Call it anti-Americanism if you will—what else could it be called? That the urge to resist Atlantis was most evident in countries, including France but also Britain and even Italy, that America had helped most to escape from Hitler's subjugation was not surprising. Where else could it be best and most readily articulated than in these leading Western democracies? To be sure, the countries of Europe, both winners and losers, were entitled to fear another war that would erupt first on their lands and would leave nothing of the little left by previous wars. Justify their anti-Americanism, therefore, as war weariness, neutralism, or pacifism. But why translate these attitudes into a full-scale indictment, literally accusing an ally of being anxious to unleash its military power on its rivals, or of exploiting its economic power to take advantage of its allies? Label it distaste, mistrust, ignorance, or envy—generalizations are difficult, as each country in Europe expressed views of its own. Yet it was there, always tainting European perceptions of American leaders and their policies and of America's history no less than its future.[14]

Nevertheless, even as such charges and rebuttals went on, political leaders throughout the victorious capitals of Europe, especially France and Britain, competed for the privileged status of America's special partner. In the new order toward which, as Italy's Foreign Minister Carlo Sforza once put it, "willingly or reluctantly, the world will in the end march," the price for such privileged status might be a bit of each nation's sovereignty—"a piece of independence" sold for "money," later wrote an embittered Vincent Auriol, first President of the French Fourth Republic.[15] Yet for countries left impoverished and weak despite victory in war, no less than for countries plunged squarely into the depth of sorrow and shame by defeat, this bargain was tempting. Moving up in the preference-scale of America's allies offered irresistible opportunities. Not only would it help reap additional Marshall Plan aid, but it would also yield greater influence over the United States and, therefore, the whole of Europe. All in all, the rewards seemed too enticing to resist.

In the competition for aid and attention, the countries of southern Europe, particularly France and Italy, complained bitterly of America's preference for countries in northern Europe, especially Britain and Germany. Paradoxically, the French and Italian trump card was their own troubling weakness: the threat posed to their postwar political regimes by large and domineering communist parties apparently ready to extend Soviet influence beyond Eastern Europe. Emphasizing their anticommunist credentials, and their relevance to U.S. interests, French and Italian leaders presented the political alternatives in their own countries in bipolar terms: a collective "we" that tied the democratic forces to their senior partner on the other side of the Atlantic, and a dismissive "they" that grouped the communists and their few political allies into a "foreign national party" under Soviet dominance. "There are only two real forces in France today, the Communists and I," de Gaulle told the U.S. ambassador to France in May 1945. And again he declared, a few months later, "If the Communists win, France will become a Soviet Republic." Italy's prime minister, Alcide de Gasperi, played the communist card no less shamelessly. "The greatest political pressure," he pointedly told Secretary of State James Byrnes in early 1947, "was being brought at this time by the communist party to bring Italy within the orbit of Russian influence."[16]

Such cynical manipulation of political realities intended to gain leverage for more U.S. aid might itself be construed as a form of latent anti-Americanism. Apparently, it worked. Once the communists were dismissed or resigned from the coalition governments they had entered in 1945, the U.S. commitment to keeping them out of power was steady. But such maneuvers only widened domestic divisions within the countries of Europe, which delayed Europe's unity, and hardened the gap between the two superpowers, which exacerbated the Continent's division.

After World War II, no state in Europe ignored the reality of its decline as rigidly and as stubbornly as Britain. Admittedly, to be sure, France could have shared the prize. As if French delusions of grandeur needed any encouragement, they were welcomed by Britain, which hoped for a confident partner on the Continent. Yet France, unlike its rival, aspired mostly to being "the first among the second class powers," as Foreign Minister Georges Bidault put it.[17] Britain, on the other hand, showed no such inhibitions. Unlike France, it had not surrendered in 1940. Having won the war made the country view itself as more than America's special partner. It made it the equal of America, since only Britain retained enough of its prewar global status and related interests and commitments to compare with that achieved by the United States after the war. Indeed, as late as March 1962—that is, almost six years after the humiliation at Suez—the *Times* could still return, approvingly, to Churchill's proud boast, "Ask what you please, look where you will, you cannot go to the bottom of the resources of Britain . . . no strain is too prolonged for the patience of our people."[18]

The limits of Britain's presumptive partnership with the United States were exposed early over such issues as President Truman's refusal to share the secrets of the atomic bomb in 1945-46, the Palestine issue in 1946-47, and the monetary debacle in 1947-48. The bad feelings these events aroused in Britain's postwar Labor government were unmistakable. "As you know all too well," wrote Sir Stafford Cripps (then the chancellor of the Exchequer) to Foreign Secretary Ernest Bevin in March 1948, the Americans "cannot look at [war and peace] calmly as we do. They always get hysterical and emotional."[19] In fact, the 1948 presidential elections in the United States threatened to bring these emotions to a head with the widely predicted victory of the conservative Republican, Thomas Dewey. Faced with the prospect of being caught between the excesses of capitalism, characteristically heaped upon the United States, and those of communism, already demonstrated by the Soviet Union, Bevin welcomed the French idea of a European third force. Without Germany (about which he was nearly as apprehensive as his French counterparts), the European house inhabited by such an odd couple might be too small. But large imperial holdings elsewhere, in Africa especially, would give it size as well as invaluable resources. And there were, too, close family ties with the Benelux countries, which, Bevin imagined, might congeal into a West European union that would include, someday, a central bank and a common currency.

Britain's interest in a close bilateral relationship with France set within a broader but limited European framework did not last long, however. Truman's surprising reelection in November 1948 served Anglo-American (and U.S.-European) relations well. Britain's socialist leaders might not have thought much of Truman, but they liked him nonetheless. They had feared that a Republican victory would restore the twin pillars of isolationism and protectionism in the United States. And at home they interpreted Dewey's defeat as a rebuke of Churchill's hard-line foreign policy and a harbinger of things to come in their own elections.[20] Four more years with Truman enhanced the appeal of the North Atlantic Treaty, which was signed in April 1949, since the credibility of the U.S. commitment was increased while the perceived risks of an imminent war with the

Soviets were reduced. A few months later, elections in Germany, which gave Konrad Adenauer and his party (in coalition with the free democrats) a slim majority over Schumacher's social democrats, isolated Britain's socialists from their partners in Europe. That made the supranational discipline of the European Coal and Steel Community unacceptable, even though its *dirigiste* flavor was otherwise compatible with the main trends in Labor's economic thinking.

As was to be shown again in later years, the construction of Europe was influenced, therefore, by the flow of domestic political elections. Who is to know what impact an ideologically hostile America, led by Dewey, and an ideologically friendly Germany, led by Schumacher, might have had in 1949 on a Labor-led Britain's relations with Europe and the United States? Suffice it to recall that Britain's rejection of an economic union with France, its opposition to the Coal and Steel Community, its dismissal of the European Defense Community, and its neglect of the EEC followed in quick succession between 1950, when the Schuman Plan was proposed, and 1955, when a Common Market was first discussed. These choices ensured that Britain's resistance to "Europe" would be as determined with Labor as with the Tories, who returned to power in October 1951.

As the Community of the Six emerged in late 1956 without London, the Community *à deux* that Britain had sought with the United States began to fade. After Suez, U.S. prestige in Britain, which had peaked during the Korean War, fell to its lowest point since the end of World War II. That the United States would appear to side with the Soviet Union against Britain (as well as France) in a region of such vital importance as the Middle East was shocking. The shock had to do with the realization that, even if acting together, the two most powerful countries in Western Europe could no longer use force without the consent and protection of the United States.[21]

The decision of Britain to join France in a battle designed to defend their complementary interests against a common threat caused a rift with the United States much sharper than the "family spat" that President Eisenhower later described in his memoirs.[22] Britain's objective was made uncharacteristically clear by Anthony Eden, who had recently replaced Churchill as prime minister. "What's all this nonsense about isolating Nasser or 'neutralizing' him . . . ? I want him destroyed. . . . I want him removed," thundered Eden early in the crisis. But such an objective, which was shared by French Premier Guy Mollet (though for different reasons), was rejected by the Eisenhower administration, which went to extraordinary lengths to quash the Anglo-French intervention. Large quantities of currency freely dumped by the U.S. Treasury in international financial markets worsened a run on the pound started by the Suez crisis. Britain's financial position made devaluation inevitable without U.S. assistance, which was made conditional on a prior cease-fire. After the cease-fire had been agreed by London, more U.S. pressure was exerted, exploiting Britain's shortage in oil supplies. Aimed at the complete withdrawal of allied forces, it forced Eden's "capitulation" in early December 1956.[23]

The reasons for the U.S. opposition to the Anglo-French action were many, including the hospitalization of the secretary of state and the 1956 presidential election, both of which crippled the administration's decision-making process during the crisis.[24] But no one reason is likely to have been as decisive as Eisenhower's own determination to prevent the escalation of this regional conflict into a global war. As explained in his memoirs, the U.S. president thought "the Soviets . . . ready to undertake any wild adventure. . . . They [were] as scared and furious as Hitler in his last days." Indeed, Eisenhower was provided with intelligence reports warning that some kind of direct Soviet military action in the Middle East was imminent.[25] This, he thought, was too high a risk to take on behalf of allies who had acted without prior consultation with the United States. And thus ended the last European attempt to act unilaterally during the Cold War.

After Suez, the French and British moved their own ways. London, anxious to mend its differences with Washington, rejected the European Community, which it continued to oppose until 1961, when a new U.S. administration persuaded Britain to change course and apply for membership in the Common Market. In France the humiliation of withdrawal from Egypt, coming two years after military defeat in Indochina, helped overcome French objections that had delayed progress in Europe since the 1955 Messina conference. In January 1957 a preliminary debate in the National Assembly on the Rome Treaty centered more on Suez and its lessons than on the treaty and its prospects. With the war in Algeria about to bring the Fourth Republic down, France's schism with America could not be bridged as readily as that between Britain and the United States. To be sure, the Suez crisis provided further evidence of Europe's dependence on the goodwill and capabilities of the United States within the context of the Atlantic community. But, as will be shown, the Suez crisis was also the catalyst that unveiled the limits of compatibility in Atlantic interests. After Suez, as Britain moved closer to the United States, France moved closer to the Federal Republic, where the main axis of the European Community began to emerge. And, in some ways, all moved away from the Atlantic Alliance from which they sought and feared distance simultaneously. Even before Suez, Chancellor Adenauer had spoken against a balance in Europe centered almost exclusively on the abundance and availability of American power. Such a balance, he warned, "must not become a permanent situation," since, he added, "vital necessities for European states are not always . . . vital necessities for the United States and vice-versa."[26] In the 1960s, the mounting problems of sustaining the Atlantic community had much to do with Europe's diminishing ambivalence about the desirability of building the European Community.

Defining the Terms of Partnership

After World War II, American policy toward Europe was guided by two aspirations: to encourage a European Community that would reduce the burden of the U.S. commitment to Europe and to promote an Atlantic community that would accommodate U.S. leadership in Europe.[27] Different as they were, these twin aspirations reflected a basic conviction that a stronger and uniting Europe and a strong and united Atlantic Alliance were not mutually exclusive. In the American view, one helped foster the other because both reinforced each other.

Why the Truman administration should have adopted the idea of Europe so quickly and unquestionably is not self-evident. There had to be more to it than a threat of Soviet subversion, since the U.S. role in promoting European unity was already firmly established during the initial planning for the Marshall Plan—at a time, that is, when the Cold War was still in its most uncertain phase. Nor was U.S. support only geared to the assumption that economic recovery would be eased in the context of integrated markets and coordinated policies, even though this assumption was made an explicit part of the Marshall proposal in May 1947. Nor, finally, was it merely a narcissistic attempt to export America's political experience to Europe, even though, no doubt, such an experience helped shape U.S. perceptions at the time. Certainly, the American commitment also grew out of the fear that unless the states of Europe were jailed into a cage forcing them to confront the evils of nationalism, the United States could not find a satisfactory solution to the security problems that, twice in thirty years, had forced it to wage war against Germany.[28]

Built in and for the Old World, the cage was to be guarded from and by the New World, at least until such time as its occupants had been rehabilitated from their former ways. Such rehabilitation, however, demanded that a measure of economic recovery and greater political stability be first attained. In 1958 this prerequisite, whose need had been recognized by Jean Monnet, was achieved by the two countries around which the European Economic Community began to form: France and the Federal Republic.[29] As Germany's economy gained even more momentum from the prosperous EEC, France regained the political strength it had lacked during the tumultuous years of the Fourth Republic. One country helped to contain and shape the other because each suspected and even feared the other's intentions.

Well served by a massive injection of Marshall Plan aid and a generous dose of U.S. protection against abusive sanctions from its victorious neighbors, the currency reform of 1948, and the integration of the Western zones in 1949, Germany's recovery was spectacular. The destruction of Germany's industrial equipment until 1945, and its dismantlement until 1951, necessitated a modernization in plants and equipment, as well as in productive methods and corporate structures, that suited the changed conditions of the divided German market and the changing conditions of the world markets. With the expanding demand that followed the outbreak of the Korean War, the undervalued deutsche mark helped stimulate German exports, thereby giving German industry ample outlets for its spare capacity. High earnings in this export-led expansion encouraged investment. Unemployment fell every year in the 1950s, but a steady flow of skilled migrants from East Germany helped stabilize the labor market, and productivity grew at a rate that permitted wage increases without inflation. Finally, security did not cost much money: military expenditures made by the occupiers proved to be an important source of revenue. All in all, Germany's economy grew at an average rate of 7.6 percent a year between 1952 and 1958, the best performance of any state that signed the Rome Treaty.[30]

Even after the Rome Treaty had been ratified by the National Assembly, France looked upon membership in a small Europe—that is, one with the Federal Republic but without Britain—with much apprehension. Since 1945 France had spoken of, and even fought for, "Europe" as the essential condition of any French role in the world. But no such role could be played without a lasting reprieve from the political instabilities that afflicted the Fourth Republic from its very beginning. This, of course, proved to be de Gaulle's foremost achievement after his return to power in May 1958—and his most enduring legacy. As he checked his nation's decline from within, he gave it the confidence needed to compete with Germany in Europe, thereby making progress toward "Europe" possible, however unwittingly.

Admittedly, de Gaulle had no tolerance for any sort of integration, whether militarily with the United States in NATO or politically with Britain in the EEC. That his resistance to both would have become especially determined after President Kennedy articulated his own vision of an integrated Atlantic community, in July 1962, should come as no surprise. As would be the case with the Nixon administration ten years later, Kennedy's call for a new Atlantic partnership was too vague where it should have been more specific but too specific where it should have remained more vague. The Europe that Kennedy (and Nixon) welcomed as an "equal partner" would have to await the hypothetical time when its members had achieved a "more perfect union" themselves, including those who, like Britain, had not yet signed the Rome Treaty. But the contributions expected from Europe did not have to be delayed as long. In asking the allies for a more generous aid program, lower trade barriers, and a coordinated approach in all economic, political, and diplomatic areas, Kennedy defined a partnership that gave Europe a more equal share of the burden but failed to provide for a more equal share of authority as well.

De Gaulle's opposition to Kennedy's vision of the future, of NATO and of the EEC, was predictable. Britain's membership in the Common Market, de Gaulle feared, would increase the U.S. presence in Europe and, therefore, Europe's dependence on the United States; hence, his sharp reaction to Prime Minister Harold Macmillan's agreement with President Kennedy at Nassau at the very end of 1962. There, in the view of the French president, Britain had reaffirmed its preference for a special relationship with the United States at the expense of a special Anglo-French relationship, which, de Gaulle believed, had been agreed several days earlier at Rambouillet.[31] Thus convinced of an Anglo-Saxon collusion aimed at his leadership at a time when he could be more directly, and even deliberately, indifferent to Atlantic unity, de Gaulle lost no more time in denying Britain's application for membership in the Common Market. The saga of Britain's entry in Europe was extended for another decade.

The general's no to Britain was not a general no to "Europe," however. Much of de Gaulle's concern—which he was hardly the only European (or French) leader to hold—had to do with the progressive erosion of national sovereignty in a supranational polity that bureaucracies and governments would be unable to stop, reverse, or even slow down. Central to any such erosion was the unanimity rule that protected the state's ability to attend to its interests and values. By refusing to devalue the supreme authority of the nation-state—"except for myths, fictions and pageants"—de Gaulle diluted the federalist dream, of course.[32] But he did not end it, and the Rome Treaty, which de Gaulle had reportedly planned to destroy, endured. In fact, it even prospered during the general's tenure, as the two years that followed de Gaulle's veto were among the most productive in the movement toward economic unity for Europe.[33]

A decade later, almost to the day, Britain's entry in the Community, along with Denmark and Ireland, coincided with, and contributed to, a marked transformation of the balance of economic power and political influence among the EC's members. For one, French economic weight in the EC, which had grown from 19.5 percent in 1960 to 23 percent in 1972, declined in the 1970s, especially relative to that of the Federal Republic.[34] As a result, the ability of the French government to impose its will on its EC partners was reduced, as could be seen first with Pompidou's attempt at monetary union, which depended on Chancellor Brandt's reluctant support, and, next, with Giscard's negotiation of the European Monetary System, which could not have succeeded without Chancellor Schmidt's acquiescence.

Nor was France's decline vis-à-vis its EC partners limited to economic factors. After de Gaulle, hopes for a rapprochement between the United States and France were short-lived. Instead, disputes between the two countries grew increasingly bitter during the Pompidou presidency, when the French vision of European unity under French leadership clashed with an especially forceful vision of Atlantic unity under U.S. leadership. In 1956 the United States had contained Europe's challenge to its leadership, and the fragmentation of the alliance, by weakening the Anglo-French axis of European cooperation. Separating the two countries not only ended their presumption that they could undertake and sustain a joint military action in the face of U.S. opposition. It also triggered political upheavals that extended beyond the political lives of Anthony Eden and Guy Mollet. The Atlantic victory thus scored by the Eisenhower administration threatened to derail Europe, as it left France alone, without Britain and with only an ascending and feared Germany to which it could turn.

In 1973 the Nixon administration defeated another European challenge to U.S. leadership, and muted the voice of Atlantic dissent, by again isolating France, this time from the Federal Republic, whose sensitivity to U.S. pressures on security issues was as well known and as compelling as Britain's earlier sensitivity to U.S. pressures on monetary issues. Yet this perceived German "betrayal" of French aspirations in and for Europe—not only over oil and the Middle East but also over such other vital issues as trade and agriculture—also left Europe helplessly divided as a Community, which neither its own members nor its main Atlantic partner seemed to take seriously.

A specifically French vision of Europe and the world was viable so long as a self-assured France could maintain a direct relationship with a divided Germany in a European Community that helped contain German ambitions, and with a powerful America in a cohesive Atlantic Alliance that also contained Soviet expansion. The European Community would help defuse the political dangers of an excessive dependence on the United States. The Atlantic Alliance helped defend against the military dangers of an exclusive reliance on France's ability to balance Soviet power. Such a prospect presented an alternative to the rigidity of the Cold War—a third pole of influence (and even some power) that might appeal to France's partners in Europe, as well as other countries in the Third World, without causing excessive resentment or apprehension from either one of the two superpowers.

With the *Ostpolitik* of Chancellor Brandt moving Germany outside French influence, however, and with the Nixon administration, too, absorbed in its own dialogue with the Soviet Union, French policies were threatened with an irrelevance that their combative spokesman, Michel Jobert, could overcome neither in circumstances of East-West negotiations in 1969-73 (dubbed détente) nor in circumstances of North-South confrontation in 1973-74 (in the name of a so-called new international economic order). In sum, de

Gaulle's consuming vision of a transformed European milieu open to French influence and supportive of French ambitions did not survive the years that followed his resignation from office. Throughout the 1970s, Germany's economic ascendancy relative to France, and the rise of Soviet military power relative to the United States undermined the conditions that had permitted de Gaulle's initial challenge to the United States and his forceful bid for Europe's leadership on behalf of France.

Enduring Balance and European Renewal

Not as involved with foreign policy as his two predecessors, Valéry Giscard d'Estaing launched his presidency with the hope that he could dust off from the Republic much of its Gaullist legacy. At home, Giscard sought to improve relations between Gaullists and socialists, which had worsened under his immediate predecessor. This meant an opening to the Left, which threatened Giscard's fragile hold on his conservative majority. Abroad, the new French president also hoped for better relations with both allies and adversaries. This meant an opening to the United States in the Atlantic Alliance, in order to contain rising Soviet power, but also an opening to Europe, in order to balance Germany. On both accounts, however, Giscard's effort was much maligned by opponents who criticized both its tone and its content. At home, the political tensions that surrounded the legislative elections of March 1978, which François Mitterrand surprisingly lost, were followed by the social malaise that preceded the presidential elections of May 1981, which Giscard lost less surprisingly. Abroad, the international crises that erupted in the late 1970s introduced "an unhappy world"—as Giscard liked to call it—that was increasingly indifferent to his, or any other, French thesis.

In the security context that framed transatlantic and intra-European relations, the sacrosanct principle of absolute deterrence within the French national sanctuary was cautiously blunted during the Giscard presidency. By making more likely France's early and more extensive participation in NATO-directed battlefield actions on West German territory (with conventional as well as with nuclear forces), Giscard brought France closer to prevailing U.S. flexible-response guidelines for countering Soviet moves against Western Europe. In accord with these guidelines the French president now managed a defense budget that favored conventional and tactical nuclear forces at the expense of the French strategic force. As a marked departure from a past inherited from de Gaulle, and preserved by Pompidou, potentially embarrassing discussions and even arrangements between French armed forces and NATO were started. In addition, plans for acquiring backup facilities on French soil (available only under specified and restricted conditions) were considered.

Although discreetly sought and implemented, these efforts were forcefully opposed by all political groups in France except for Giscard's own small centrist party. Nor did they do much to gain Giscard the support of French allies, especially in the United States, where the attention of the Carter administration remained focused on the French reluctance to engage in open criticism of Soviet actions in Afghanistan and elsewhere or to follow the American lead in the Middle East. Now cloaked in a tailored Gaullist mantle, Mitterrand and his socialist allies condemned harshly the prospect of an "extended sanctuary" that might cause France's early participation in a battle of Germany. Plans involving the use of France's tactical nuclear weapons, they argued in 1980-81, would extend the process of escalation, detract from absolute national deterrence, and involve France in unacceptable defensive actions.[35] Inherently credible, such criticism from the dominant opposition party caused renewed apprehensions that a socialist regime in France would return to pre-Giscardian Gaullist strategic and force-structure guidelines. They also prompted concerns that French relations with NATO, which had begun to improve under Giscard, would move back toward the more explicitly adversarial status carved out by de Gaulle in 1966, without restoring the cooperative Franco-German dimension he had achieved simultaneously.[36]

Yet, after he won the 1981 presidential elections, Mitterrand returned to his earlier Atlantic and European vocations, those that had earned him Jean Monnet's confidence as *"une valeur sûre"* the first time he had sought the presidency in 1965.[37] In so doing, Mitterrand responded to the same external factors that had motivated Giscard: the risk of Soviet military superiority in Europe and Germany's future in such a Soviet-dominated Europe. Thus, by providing support for a NATO-missile deployment on German territory, Mitterrand helped counter, at no cost to France, the deployment of Soviet SS-20s, whose precision and multiple-warhead capability directly threatened French strategic and industrial targets. By helping Chancellor Schmidt defeat his own party's opposition to the deployment of new NATO missiles on German soil, the French president also aimed to counter a German drift toward neutralism deemed dangerous to Europe and, hence, to the security of France.

Mitterrand's assist, peaking with his celebrated speech at the *Bundestag* in January 1983, was especially significant because neither he personally nor his party or even his country was known for exaggerated assessments of Soviet military power on behalf of NATO. Well served by this unexpected display of French support—but also helped by an incompetent Soviet leadership, the politically attractive double-zero proposal of late 1981 on intermediate-range nuclear forces (INF), and the impressive performance of the American economy after the difficult recession of 1981-82—the INF compromise demonstrated a unity that the Atlantic Alliance had not enjoyed in a generation. At the 1983 Williamsburg summit of industrial countries agreement over a wide range of other political and economic issues confirmed that the Atlantic discord, which had been amply in evidence during and immediately after the 1982 Versailles meeting, had been settled.

The European policy of the pre-Gaullist years was resurrected in 1983-85, following a bitter internal debate over the constraints forced upon a socialist France by the restrictive institutions and practices of a European Monetary System dominated by the Federal Republic. The failure of three successive devaluations of the franc between October 1981 and March 1983 seemed conclusive at last: changes in the French economy since the similar (but highly effective) steps taken by de Gaulle and Pompidou in 1958 and 1969 could no longer be ignored. With growing insufficiencies in equipment goods, resulting from fifteen years of steady neglect of industrial investment (which fell from 13.5 percent of the gross national product in 1973 to 10.3 percent in 1987), each unit of industrial production in France now contained about 85 percent of imports, as compared with less than 60 percent for West Germany. In the early 1980s, therefore, the more the socialists devalued, the more the French trade deficit with Germany soared, rising from 17 billion French francs in 1980 to 44 billion francs in 1986.

The limits of national autonomy had been approached at last. A franc kept stable and strong within the confining structure of the German-dominated EMS, which Giscard had helped organize, might cost jobs, which it did, and even growth. But it would also permit lower inflation and, in the long run, the lower interest rates required for the development of support industries that could reduce French reliance on imported equipment goods. Faced at the time with other such self-reinforcing factors as increasingly assertive German and Soviet policies, which severely constrained France's foreign policy options, Mitterrand's European journey was resumed *faute de mieux*. It was the only available alternative to the two models that had been envisaged under the Fifth Republic. "France cannot be France without grandeur," de Gaulle had often said. "Europe cannot be Europe without socialism," Mitterrand had often argued. Now that the French president had abandoned his party's pretense of a rupture with capitalism, he was ready to move toward the more modest vision of a France that could be France without socialism, and even without grandeur, but not without Europe: "France is my country," the president declared on January 15, 1987, "and Europe is our future."

Echoes of the Fourth Republic: as the European Defense Community had been proposed as a means of arming German soldiers without reorganizing the German army, a European Monetary Union would now rely on the deutsche mark without relinquishing all authority to the *Bundesbank*, after a short interlude during which the European Monetary System had permitted both. Thus, even before events around and within Europe began to move at a pace that Mitterrand would not have dared hope for—and, perhaps, not dared fear either—the French president was placing Germany at the center of a grand strategy designed to move "Europe" *tous azimuts.*

Significantly enough, however, in so doing the French president did not attempt to displace the United States from the Continent. On the contrary, the relaunching of the European Community that began with the 1984 Fontainebleau summit was inspired by the perceived need to follow an American model that appeared to have regained its vigor at home and its assertiveness abroad. Mitterrand's criticism of "Europe's silence" in the midst of the then-evolving changes in U.S.-Soviet relations was resumed later: first as a delayed reaction to the 1984 summit in Reykjavík, when, he complained, decisions vital to the security of Europe were considered by the two super-powers without consultation with their allies;[38] and next after the 1991 Gulf War, when the French government resumed its quest for a European identity in the area of defense.

In an ironic reversal of roles, Margaret Thatcher's opposition to Mitterrand's initiatives in and about Europe echoed de Gaulle's rhetoric about the eternal realities of the nation-state threatened by the fiction of an appointed bureaucracy in Brussels. "France as France, Spain as Spain, Britain as Britain, each with its own customs, traditions and identity," harped Thatcher at Bruges on September 20, 1988. "I really was very much in agreement with de Gaulle," she had said a few weeks earlier, "that this is a Europe of separate countries working together."[39] In May 1962 de Gaulle, too, had dismissed a Europe "thought and written in some integrated esperanto or volapuk" as a fiction oblivious to the reality of "France with its French, Germany with its Germans, Italy with its Italians."[40] The French president, who had liked neither Britain's insularity (which he nevertheless envied at times) nor the British people (whose solidarity under duress he sadly contrasted with the divisions of the French people), would have applauded Thatcher's rhetoric no less than her obstinacy.

Thatcher's apprehensions, therefore, were neither unheard of in Europe nor without foundation in British policy. For Thatcher, as for her predecessors, and for their colleagues in other countries, objecting to the application of texts and arrangements that might not fulfill the nation's interests was hardly inappropriate and did not mean a death warrant for "Europe," or even a stay of execution. To pretend otherwise would be to place the blame for failure and delays not on circumstances and the very complexity of the process involved but on a succession of villains who betrayed the spirit of that process. In the construction of "Europe," as in the conduct of international relations generally, the definition of villainy is a task that is almost always hopeless and often meaningless. In most cases it is seldom clear whether behavior is a reflection of circumstances or intentions, of the coming of wisdom or the evidence of failure.

In 1954 France's Pierre Mendès-France, for example, was said to be a "bad" European who "killed" Europe because of his opposition to the EDC; yet within a few months came the Western European Union, which the French prime minister approved. In 1964 Georges Pompidou, then de Gaulle's prime minister, was not a "bad" European because he explicitly threatened to end the Community lest the Common Agricultural Policy, be completed within the time limits set by the Council of Ministers; within a few years, as France's new president, he set the stage for a monetary *relance* that dared envision monetary union soon and political union in another ten years. In 1975 Helmut Schmidt was not a "bad" European driven by a visceral dislike for the Commission and its agricultural policy; soon afterward, his leadership produced a European Monetary System that revived Pompidou's failed project for monetary union. Nor, in the late 1980s, was Thatcher merely another "bad" European who tried to disrupt the single economic market or unravel economic and monetary union.

"There is one thing," an exasperated Jean Monnet once told his interlocutors in London, "you British will never understand: an idea. And there is one thing you are supremely good at grasping: a hard fact. We will have to make Europe without you—but then you will have to come in and join us."[41] Spaak, as mentioned earlier, had used similar language. Like Spaak, Monnet was hardly proved wrong, as Britain's opposition to Europe remained consistent without ever turning permanent. But Monnet's anger should not have been confined to Britain. The implementation of any idea may demand a different timing for everyone who subscribes to it. Britain's delay in joining Europe has never been a matter of party alignments or political personalities. Clement Attlee declined to join the ECSC in 1950, Winston Churchill dismissed the EDC in 1952, Anthony Eden ignored the Rome Treaty in 1956, Harold Macmillan diluted Britain's first bid to join the EEC in 1961, Harold Wilson objected to the terms of membership in 1974, and James Callaghan declined to enter the Exchange Rate Mechanism (ERM) of the European Monetary System in 1979. In October 1990 Thatcher's belated decision to join the ERM confirmed Monnet's principle: in the end, no one, probably including the prime minister herself, was truly surprised by her decision to bring Britain at last into the mechanism against which she had fought for so long. She, after all, understood a fact.

That the most compelling British prime minister since Winston Churchill—one who stood over the national and European scenes in as dominant a fashion as de Gaulle had twenty years earlier—would have been defeated primarily on the issue of Britain's role in Europe will not be easily forgotten by any of her successors. For even as she took on the European Community, Thatcher looked politically invincible. Unemployment in Britain rose above two million in 1980, for the first time since 1935; race riots erupted in most major cities (including London, Liverpool, and Birmingham) in 1981; war raged in the South Atlantic over the Falkland Islands in 1982; the miners' strike brought despair and anger in 1984; unemployment continued to rise in 1985; a string of bitter resignations from her cabinet began as early as 1986, in the key ministries of defense and, shortly afterward, trade. Nevertheless, through it all, Thatcher's stature grew: every battle she waged she won, until 1987 when her political dominance and her ability to govern appeared to peak.

Within the Conservative Party, underneath the passionate clash of personal ambitions, Britain's commitment to, and role in, Europe was the catalyst for the passionate leadership struggle that began with Michael Heseltine's resignation from the cabinet in early 1986 and ended dramatically in late 1990. Absent any other issue that might have helped Thatcher's political opponents unite in order to win the leadership they sought, the more the prime minister voiced her dislike for Europe, the more other conservative leaders showed interest in it. As such a battle unfolded, the Labor Party also discovered Europe in spite of itself. Like other such parties in southern Europe, Labor, too, would have preferred to build socialism on its own terms—terms, that is, that Labor outlined when it managed the heated referendum in 1975 over Britain's entry in the EEC and when it lost the premiership in 1979. But after Labor's preference for a "gentle rupture" with capitalism had been dismissed in Britain's general elections of 1983, the more Thatcher criticized Europe, the more her opponents learned to praise it.

"The insularity of the English," George Orwell once observed, "their refusal to take foreigners seriously, is a folly that has to be paid very heavily from time to time."[42] Throughout the saga of community-building in Europe, Britain's folly has been to argue its way into the impasse of resignation from, and abdication to, a European idea that, for more than four decades, its governments have fought as a fact of history and joined as a fact of life. Paradoxically, Thatcher's main contribution to the idea of Europe, like de Gaulle's, may well have been that she at last ended the folly of believing that "Europe" could be ignored at no cost to the country and its leaders.

But hers has not been the only folly that shaped Europe's journey throughout the Cold War. At first, the United States exerted an influence that was repeatedly decisive: helpful but firm when the process moved in a direction that accommodated American objectives, as was mostly the case during the years of the Truman administration; threatening but still constructive when it was mired in a stalemate that might harm American policies, as was the case during the early years of the Eisenhower administration. At the beginning of the 1960s, however, the process acquired enough momentum to make new American summons for European unity unnecessary and potentially counterproductive. U.S. responses to "Europe" now became more equivocal and even, on occasion, obtrusive. It was not long before the many parochial nationalisms that had populated postwar Europe were remembered to have been more manageable than the larger and stronger "European" nationalism that was taking their place. This recollection of an easier past was enough to stir ambivalence in the United States about a future that appeared less and less congenial as Europe's unity became more and more irreversible.

President Kennedy's interest in a new Atlantic partnership confirmed this ambivalence. As the EEC engaged in its first round of tariff cuts, it spoke increasingly with a voice that lacked the Atlantic accent America had come to expect. The West, Kennedy had complained in his 1961 State of the Union Address, was "unfulfilled and in some disarray, . . . weakened by economic rivalry and partially eroded by national interest[s]." The closer Atlantic partnership urged by the U.S. president in July 1962 was presented as a bold attempt to redefine a structure that had already achieved its first postwar objectives: political stability, economic recovery, and even some measure of military security. However, delaying change until such time as Europe had defined itself made it possible to maintain the status quo in the Atlantic community for some time, without accelerating the emergence of a European community. In any case, within a few months, the Cuban missile crisis reminded the allies of the enduring reality of the U.S.-Soviet confrontation, and, de Gaulle notwithstanding, it confirmed U.S. leadership in an area, that of military security, where the EEC remained irrelevant.

In April 1973 the Nixon administration launched an initiative under the misleading name of "Year of Europe." By that time détente with the Soviet Union, normalization with the People's Republic of China, and peace negotiations in Vietnam were all well under way. After many years of emphasis on the resolution of adversary relations, improvement of alliance relations was, therefore, overdue. In the Atlantic community there was a widespread sense that the Cold War was abating at a time when neither superpower appeared to be either willing or able to sustain its rivalry with the other. Moreover, the European Community was in an ascending mood: the previous year in Paris its members had pledged to complete their political union by 1980, by which time some publicly dared to anticipate a European government.

With America's main partner looking into the future with such confidence, the moment for a "fresh act of creation" that—in Kissinger's words—would be "equal to that undertaken by the postwar generations of leaders of Europe and America" seemed propitious. That it ended with unprecedented acrimony reflected the growing gap between the European perception of an American partner whose power was relatively diminished and less needed than in the past and the American perception of a European influence that had become relatively greater and more needed than had been the case in earlier years. In other words, at a time when the Atlantic community required, in the view of its American leader, that the European Community be more receptive to its needs, the European Community, in the view of its members, found the Atlantic community less relevant to its own.

Given such perceptions, Kissinger appeared eager to give Europe added responsibility for any of the "new problems" he feared but determined to leave America with unlimited access to any "new opportunities" he expected from the global changes he had uncovered. The true objective of the Year of Europe proposal, it was argued by some Europeans, was to weaken their position in the forthcoming trade negotiations, the Tokyo Round, and to divide European states and fragment European institutions in order to absorb them all into a U.S.-dominated supra-Atlantic area.[43] These circumstances and the responses that followed echoed those that had surrounded Kennedy's call in 1962, on the eve of the Kennedy Round of trade negotiations. In any case, before the argument could gather force, the first oil crisis intervened, and Europe's disarray on vital security issues was displayed once again.

The Vision Thing

Examples of U.S. opposition to European initiatives abound. They make it possible to dismiss or neglect America's role in guiding Europe's journey during the Cold War. Whatever transatlantic and intra-European discord this opposition may have caused, however, its impact was not destructive of the Atlantic personality it sought to protect or of the European identity it resisted. For in the end, the vision originally outlined by the Truman administration succeeded because, and not in spite, of the ways in which it was organized and defended by all of Truman's successors—and often in spite, and usually not because, of the indiscriminate criticism addressed by European leaders and their constituents to every U.S. president, each of whom was charged with saying and doing too much or too little.

In the 1960s, for example, de Gaulle's declarations gave the world a glimpse of a future—Europe from the Atlantic to the Urals—that would have to be sought without, and even against, U.S. leadership. De Gaulle was hailed as a visionary who anticipated the end of the Cold War and the end of Europe's division. But would that future—later described by Mikhail Gorbachev as a "common European house"—have come within reach had the American leadership not continued to be exerted, against and without de Gaulle? The vision he had of the future was not so visionary after all. His concern with the U.S.-Soviet condominium that would follow "détente, cooperation, and entente" hardly materialized when the end of the Cold War took place on terms close to a Soviet surrender with (nearly) no conditions. To argue now that the French president was right twenty years too early is to misunderstand, or misrepresent, the specifics of his evocation of the future. In any case, what is the point of being right twenty years too early—if not of having been wrong for twenty years too many?

In responding to the French challenges of those years the moderation shown by the Kennedy and Johnson administrations was no small achievement. Especially over France's departure from NATO, a public outburst might have worsened relations between the two countries even further and caused additional damage to the Western alliance at a critical time.[44] Who is to say, then, that had the United States succumbed to the French pressures, the related objectives of integration (Western Europe), unification (Germany), liberation (Eastern Europe), and containment (USSR) would have been fulfilled as quickly, and as peacefully, as they were twenty-one years after de Gaulle's political retirement (and, in a nice historical touch, on the one hundredth anniversary of his birth)? Who is to pretend that without the outspoken and multidimensional challenge issued by the Reagan administration to the Soviet Union in the early 1980s—against the preference shown by the countries of Europe for a more conciliatory and even, indeed, more appeasing tone—a new Soviet leadership would have accepted defeat and acquiesced to change later in the decade?

The reluctance often shown by the European allies in following American leadership throughout the Cold War should not distract attention from the fact that notwithstanding the repeated charges of vacillations against that leadership, it still demonstrated remarkable continuity and success. What has been at stake over the years, and what remains at stake now, is not merely the ambivalence that the United States has shown toward "Europe" but also the ambivalence that the states of Europe, including, but not limited to, France, have shown toward both "Europe" and the United States.

All too often political leaders on both sides of the Atlantic have found it convenient to blame their allies and their neighbors for the difficulties they faced at home by exaggerating the realities of transatlantic and intra-European differences on a large variety of political, economic, and military issues. Resulting charges and countercharges flowing from Europe to the United States, and vice versa, gave both the Alliance and Europe a tone of discord that drowned out, on occasion, the continued reality of cooperation in and between the two related communities. More than once the Alliance was declared dead, and when deemed still alive, it was always found irreparably damaged—cracked, troubled, unhinged, or fading. Concomitantly, "Europe" was readily dismissed, even by its own adherents—declared to be astray, declining, or Finlandized at any moment in the present; about to be bargained away, in need of shelter, buffered, or isolated as a fortress at any moment in the future.

Yet neither the gloomy analyses of the moment nor the dire predictions about the future came to pass. In 1989-90 the success of

American leaders in defeating their post-World War II adversary (and containing the fears of their allies) and the success of European leaders in defeating their historical ghosts (and managing the exasperation of their protector) argued for both the preservation of the transatlantic alliance and the pursuit of intra-European integration. Ultimately, the only special relationship that truly endured the test of time was not between any two or three states across the Atlantic or within Europe, but one between the two sides of the Atlantic—namely, between an America that became steadily Europeanized during the Cold War and a Europe that may finally become Americanized in the wake of the Cold War. Therein, far in the future, lies the community of transatlantic interests imagined by Kennedy as the natural outgrowth of the postwar vision of U.S.-European relations that guided Truman's rhetoric and motivated Eisenhower's action.

3
Sculpting a Community

S tarted amidst the ruins inherited from two world wars, the unification of Western Europe proceeded haltingly during the years of the Cold War, as nation-states sought to preserve to different degrees whatever might remain of their autonomy and identity. No project was ever completed on time and fully, as every state, predictably, sought to avoid or to pass on to others the internal pains demanded in the name of European unity. Yet every delay carried with it the seeds of the new beginning that followed, and every advance in one area prepared the ground for new initiatives elsewhere. When this process ends at last, there will be some truth to the claim that "Europe" was constructed in a fit of absent-mindedness—without, that is, a concrete vision of, or an explicit commitment to, the integrated community that was ultimately unveiled.

The process of European unity can most clearly be viewed, and, hence, be taken most seriously, from a multiyear perspective that escapes the day-to-day disappointments of incomplete agreements and unfulfilled promises. Considered at any one time, and examined in the light of any one issue, "Europe" can be legitimately dismissed as a failure. Negotiations over the least significant item drag on, seemingly indefinitely. Alibis for inaction are amply available. Divisions cause conflicts, and conflicts produce new delays. Observed from a narrow focus, the obstacles to progress always seem too large and unsurmountable. But seen in the light of what has already been achieved, the gloom of the moment fades as it becomes also all too clear that no setback on the path to unity has ever been final.

Turning the clock of European progress a few decades back suffices to confirm the hopes entertained by the EC countries, each, as de Gaulle once put it, "with its own spirit, its own history, its own language, its own misfortunes, glories, and ambitions."[1] Every new loss of sovereignty may well tempt each nation-state to withdraw from a Community that ignores, and even overrides, its particular interests. Yet, however much an EC state is denied progressively a life of its own, each is now condemned to cohabitate permanently with its partners, however reluctantly it may have joined the Community initially. On both economic and political grounds, too, no European state outside the Community can fail to seek membership, however justified its reluctance may have been in previous years. "Europe" has much room for expansion but none for contraction.

The Politics of Economic Integration

The idea of Europe showed its first institutional gain in April 1948 with the formation of the Organization for European Economic Cooperation (OEEC). Launched a few months before the first postwar economic recession (which began in the United States in late 1948), the new organization envisioned a new and striking form of international cooperation. Divisions among ex-allies, ex-enemies, and ex-neutrals ran deep, and the needs faced by all were substantial. Strategies based on planned economies in Britain, Holland, and the Scandinavian countries, a free market in Belgium, and unevenly mixed economies in France and Italy generated a plethora of conflicting ideas for recovery. These economic strategies, in turn, reflected important political differences from country to country and made coordination even more difficult to imagine. In this context, believing that there could be agreement on a fair distribution of the much-needed Marshall Plan aid demanded an act of faith that only the United States could perform.

The French, determined to maintain a vigilant control on the reconstruction of their defeated enemy, Germany, pressed for a strong and even supranational organization that would attend to this supervision collectively (but without German representation). The British, on the other hand, preferred a weaker and broader organization that, extended to the United States, could be influenced more readily than the more narrow European organization favored by France. Some members agreed with the U.S. objective of creating a single internal market for all OEEC members. Others proposed instead to organize smaller common markets limited to two, three, or five countries under mysterious names that merged the names of their participants: Francita for France and Italy; Benelux for Belgium, the Netherlands, and Luxemburg; and Finebel for all five.

The point is that, in the absence of any real option, this first tentative step toward European unity was hardly a matter of choice. Nor was it a matter of shared ideals, of which there seemed to be a dearth in Europe, however such ideals might be described. The OEEC was a piece of ad hoc machinery imposed upon reluctant European states by a determined American benefactor who insisted firmly that the distribution of its desperately needed aid be managed on a joint basis. Yet, undaunted by the political taint of overt U.S. pressure, "true" Europeanists fervently believed that the OEEC would continue to function after the completion of Europe's economic rehabilitation, when it might even be invested with some political power.[2]

In August 1949 the Council of Europe provided a first indication that the search for unity in Europe would be multidimensional—economic, of course, but political as well. While the OEEC dealt with economic cooperation, the Council was organized in Strasbourg to facilitate political cooperation through a parliamentary Consultative Assembly and a semipermanent Committee of Ministers. Joined by only ten of the sixteen OEEC members, the Council also gave an early indication of the multispeed character of European unity. Countries would join in their own time, and all European institutions would not have the same membership at any one time. As it turned out, the Council's general irrelevance to the momentous political events of those years confirmed that the states of Europe, whatever their number, preferred to maintain strict limits on the scope and pace of their cooperation, whatever its nature and purpose.

"Of all the international bodies I have known," Paul-Henry Spaak, the first president of the European Assembly, once thundered, "I have never found any more timorous or more impotent."[3] He was right. The Council's structure satisfied mostly Britain's preference for a deliberative body that had neither centralized authority (as the French postwar predilection for supranational European institutions might have entailed), nor even diffuse democratic legitimacy: since it excluded communist representation, the Council could not even be seen as fully representative of its members. Indeed, its grand rhetoric notwithstanding, the Assembly became so aware of the limitations placed on its mandate that, as early as 1951, its parliamentarians voted to confine their deliberations to the less significant, and thus least contentious, questions.[4]

Although new steps on behalf of European integration followed quickly, these steps were not initiated by the Council in Strasbourg but by the French government in Paris, and not because of any commitment to "Europe" but because of continued apprehensions about Germany. It was there, in Germany, that the French postwar thesis—no German control of its own coal and steel resources (which was dismissed by the United States), and the Anglo-Saxon antithesis—no indefinite discrimination against any Western country (which was feared on the Continent), merged to produce the European Coal and Steel Community (ECSC), an imaginative European synthesis calling for the abdication of national control by all members. Barely hidden behind its glowing references to the construction of Europe lurked the French interest in strong organizations with supranational authority over German resources. Already twice defeated by the weak structures and mandates of the OEEC and the Council of Europe, this interest now applied to a sector of vital relevance to defense policy. The French objective was not only unmistakable but also nonnegotiable: to impose irreversible restrictions on the sovereignty of its most persistent adversary in modern times. "The aim of this proposal," French Foreign Minister Robert Schuman bluntly told Chancellor Konrad Adenauer, "is not economic but highly political." Its purpose was to enable the member-states "to discern the first signs of any . . . rearmament," which, in those days, would most likely begin with an increase in coal, iron, and steel production.[5]

Nor was this all. As with other French schemes for and about "Europe," *les grandes affaires* merged with narrower economic interests. In 1949 France's production in crude steel amounted to 9 million tons, more than in any year since 1929. With plans to expand production by 6 million tons by 1953, export markets were needed, and the French feared competition from a rising steel output in the Ruhr. French coal production, on the other hand, was lagging behind. Although production was high, equipment good, and output per manshift well above the European average, France still relied on imports that came mostly from the Ruhr region. Thus the Schuman Plan was expected to help France on steel exports as well as coal imports—a matter of no small significance, too, for the Saar, a heavy producer of both steel and coal and a territory the French had attempted to separate from Germany by demanding that it join the Council of Europe as an associate member. Yet this first allocation of supranational authority to a European executive body, with powers and revenues of its own, was not achieved with ease. In late 1950 Adenauer's initial enthusiasm for the French plan, which he had welcomed primarily on political grounds, was so blunted by the opposition of German industrialists that the French government found it necessary to call on the Truman administration for help in getting the treaty signed in April 1951.

Despite Britain's refusal to join an organization that not only would be European and supranational but would also clash with the postwar nationalization of its coal industry, this start was promising. It showed how hereditary fears that might not be overcome between the European states could be addressed among them, in the name of a fiction called "Europe." It was this fiction that would permit a fusion of national power based on a commonality of interests. That such a European fiction would be especially appealing to the United States was of no small advantage, since it also fostered the Atlantic reality required for the Continent's recovery and security.

On the question of European unity, the U.S. view had already been made explicit. National sovereignty could not be qualified for any one state alone, a prospect the French were willing to entertain at Germany's expense, but it could be restricted for all states, a course the United States advocated for the benefit of all. But now, with the ECSC, the quest for European unity along lines favored by the United States was resumed as the result of an initiative inspired by the Europeans. This was an achievement of no small significance. While it escaped the ad hocery of the OEEC, it also confirmed a willingness on the Continent to embark on a journey for which the United States could not have remained indefinitely the sole guide.

In September 1950 French plans for the European Defense Community (EDC) outlined a similar compromise, though one enormously more ambitious, between Western needs for security against the Soviet Union and European concerns over pressing U.S. pleas for the rearmament of Germany. As had been the case with the Coal and Steel Community, "Europe" would provide access to, but deny national control over, needed German resources: the German soldiers demanded by the United States on behalf of Western defense, but without the German national army opposed most openly by France in the name of Europe's security. The security system that was then envisioned at the start of the Cold War, would attend to the double containment of Soviet imperialism and German militarism with two indivisible communities, one Atlantic and the other European, that confirmed the rise of America as a European power and the fall of Germany as a divided country.

Differently from country to country, but significantly in each, four main concerns shaped the intra-European debate that followed: that the EDC would resurrect the German army; that it would destroy other national armies; that it would erode the sovereignty of the nation-state in the vital area of national defense; and that it would precipitate a European political community for which the projected member-states were not prepared, with or without U.S. participation. The project could have worked, however. In June 1950 the Soviet-sponsored North Korean invasion of South Korea was seen as the harbinger of things to come elsewhere. Most generally, the Europeans feared that the war might divert U.S. capabilities and will away from Europe and toward a region that was of marginal interest to them. After China's entry in the war, they also feared a Soviet military intervention that might cause a spillover of the conflict into Europe. In effect, led by Britain, they insisted that no further escalation take place without consultation and agreement with them, including, especially, the use of the atomic bomb—a demand that the Truman administration would not meet explicitly, despite urgent public pressures from London and Paris.[6]

More specifically, the European allies feared that events in an artificially divided Korea might be repeated in and over a divided Germany. Whatever differences there might be between the two countries, the parallels were all too obvious. In contrast with the relatively benign assessments that had prevailed before the summer of 1950, the Soviet threat now appeared so ominous, and Western capabilities so inadequate, as to justify and even require a European initiative whose scope, coming only five years after the end of World War II, was truly extraordinary.

Charged with deterring the dangers raised by both an aggressively expansionist Soviet Union and a potentially revanchiste German state, the guarantee provided by the United States through the North Atlantic Treaty of April 1949 no longer seemed sufficient: the containment of Soviet expansion required a sizable deployment of U.S. forces. If Germany's rearmament was to be made a precondition for this deployment, as Dean Acheson insisted in September 1950, so be it. At most, his insistence confirmed the European perceptions of an American innocence in world affairs that needed to be corrected with a bit of French imagination, British diplomacy, and Italian ambiguity. But even the presumed ignorance of U.S. leaders did not negate the necessity of securing a tangible presence of American power in Europe, and it was to accommodate such a necessity that the French proposed the European Defense Community as a means for rearming Germany. To the extent that it was intended to reconcile the American demands with Continental needs, the EDC was a serious European proposal meant to resolve a serious problem. To this extent, too, the Truman administration, which understood the French motives, was ready to accept that rearmament take place outside the Atlantic framework it favored. Only later, as the EDC debate dragged on, did the Eisenhower administration come close to proceeding with Germany's rearmament without France, a step that might have meant the collapse of both the European Community and NATO.[7]

Four years of bitter intra-European and transatlantic debates followed the French proposal. Argument centered on Britain's participation and the reliability of America's guarantees. Britain's refusal to join the proposed Community, and America's reluctance to press for British membership (as forcefully, and hence, as decisively as was done for the European Economic Community a few years later) went beyond the issue of common defense. It expressed a broader rebuttal of Europe as a self-sufficient and autonomous unit. Europe, declared Britain's Foreign Secretary Bevin in November 1950, at a time when the EDC was still politically viable, "is not enough; it is not big enough, it is not strong enough, and it is not able to stand by itself."[8]

Bevin's emphasis on the limits of European power, and, therefore, on the limits of a European identity in the unsafe environment created by the Cold War, was comprehensible. Yet the EDC, in its initial conception, was not only about the integration of military forces in Western Europe. It was also about a U.S.-sponsored framework that would add to the European identity defined by the EDC an Atlantic personality dominated by the United States, and without which the combined objectives of absorbing Germany and containing the Soviet Union could not be fulfilled. That the French welcomed this broader Atlantic context could be seen in their efforts to assimilate their own colonial war in Indochina to the American war in Korea, described in Paris as the same war against the same enemy, waged for the same cause and with the same sacrifices.[9] French perceptions of both communities, and of France's role in either, quickly evolved, however, and such claims were not repeated a few years later in Algeria.

By August 1954, when a moribund EDC was finally buried in the French National Assembly, the first U.S.-Soviet détente that followed Stalin's death in March 1953—including the end of the Korean War in July—had already reduced East-West tensions and assuaged the European anxieties that had prompted the French offer for an integrated defense community. By that time, too, fears of communist subversion in the West were beginning to subside, especially in France and Italy, where the local communist parties appeared no longer able to return to the coalition governments that they had left, or been dismissed from, in May 1947. Even Eisenhower's threat of an agonizing reappraisal of America's alliance commitments, and the diplomatic confusion caused among Western countries by the belated rejection of the EDC by its prime sponsor, did not last. In October 1954 the thorny problem of military integration was moved by Britain into the Western European Union (WEU) which expanded an organization sketched in the 1948 Brussels Treaty. As France agreed to a general Western structure built with, rather than against, a divided Germany (which also pledged nuclear abstinence), Britain made its most explicit commitment to the defense of Europe. After the Federal Republic's formal admission into the North Atlantic Treaty Organization in May 1955, the WEU, whose main purpose had been to restore the pretense of European unity in order to salvage the reality of Atlantic unity, was forgotten (at least for the next three decades), and the process of European integration, threatened with a death warrant after the collapse of the EDC, soon resumed with more modest calls for a common market.

The Economics of Political Unity

In March 1957 the Rome Treaty launched the European Economic Community (EEC). The most immediate purpose of the EEC was to create a common market that would gradually abolish tariffs and other obstructions to trade from within and establish a common external tariff on imports from nonmember countries for the world without. Yet, from the beginning, the EEC aimed at much more than a customs union, as it anticipated closer political union among its members (France and Germany, as well as Italy and the Benelux countries). Such an ultimate objective, it was surmised, could be fulfilled more effectively with the relatively small economic steps the EEC proposed—which "seemed rather vague" to the like of Monnet—than with the politico-military grand designs for a United States of Europe that had been devised in previous years.[10]

After the broad terms of the Rome Treaty had been outlined at the Messina conference in June 1955, the political and economic conditions for a quick agreement on the preparation and ratification of the projected economic community were particularly propitious. If anything, in 1955 and 1956 many of the postwar divisions of Western Europe appeared to be ending. With the termination of the Occupation Statute, the Federal Republic was accepted by its European partners as a rearmed and sovereign member of the Western Alliance. With the conclusion of the protracted debate over the European Defense Community, Britain made a historically unprecedented commitment to the military security of Europe, one that also carried significant political implications. And, finding in Britain's commitment the needed counterweight to German power, France, too, seemed willing to complete the triangular partnership that would give Europe a springboard from which to leap forward into a new future.

Moreover, the political coalitions that had defeated the EDC in 1953-54 seemed in retreat throughout Europe. In France the January 1956 elections produced a European and Atlanticist majority led by a moderate socialist party in coalition with the christian democrats. Later that year, the Soviet intervention in Hungary split the Italian Left, thereby starting the political compromise that brought the Italian Socialist Party into the governing majority led by the christian democrats a few years later. Finally, in Germany the 1957 elections strengthened Chancellor Adenauer's majority and left the social democrats with no alternative but to join the national consensus defined by the christian democrats.

The economic *relance* of the early 1950s also made the European political *relance* of 1955-56 especially timely. The mean growth rate of industrial production in the six EEC countries amounted to 8 percent a year from 1950 to 1953, and it climbed to 10 percent from 1953 to 1956.[11] As intra-European trade doubled during the six years that followed the establishment of the OEEC, the countries of Europe were coming up against monetary and trade barriers that had to be overcome. To a large extent, it was this economic vigor that made it possible for the Six to contemplate the organization of a common market among them, even though, admittedly, the fear that economic conditions might take a turn for the worse also made the member-states act quickly in 1957.[12]

In late 1956 Western disarray in the Middle East provided another catalyst for ratification, as it yielded the first compelling evidence that vital security interests might not always be viewed similarly by all members of the Atlantic Alliance. In Paris, as mentioned earlier, the preliminary debate in the National Assembly on the Rome Treaty centered more on the general lessons of the Anglo-French debacle at Suez than on the specific terms of the treaty. Unanswered threats from Moscow and irresistible pressures from Washington added up to a demonstration of impotence that strengthened the case for European unity.[13] At issue was Europe's ability to enforce its own policies in the absence of U.S. support. If France and Britain together could not do so against a military power as weak as Nasser's Egypt, and on behalf of economic and political interests as vital as access to oil and the defense of empire, what other European state, acting alone or in combination with another, could? Although the community organized by the Rome Treaty had been deliberately kept economic—a common market free of trade barriers, in which goods, services, labor, and capital could move without hindrance among the member-states—the inner logic that inspired the treaty's ratification was, therefore, fundamentally political.

Skepticism toward the EEC's ability to fulfill either its economic objectives or its political ambitions was widespread, however. Dropouts among the starting six members were more likely than the admission of new members. In France, one of the likely dropouts, the alternative to regional unity remained national grandeur, which de Gaulle was soon to preach. In Britain, one of the unlikely new members, the alternative to national impotence was not an elusive European Community but a closer partnership with the more reliable Atlantic community. Accordingly, the instrument Britain chose to defeat the Common Market with was the OEEC, the U.S.-sponsored organization that it had opposed initially. Now, the British government proposed the dismantlement of all OEEC tariffs on industrial goods as a means of gaining access inside the common tariff wall erected by the Six. Since all members of this free trade area for industrial goods would keep their own tariffs against non-OEEC countries, Britain's industrial exports would gain duty-free access to the Common Market on the Continent while its food and raw material imports continued to benefit from the preferential system with the Commonwealth countries.[14]

The broader free trade area urged by London depended for its success on Germany's adhesion. Clearly, the German government would have preferred a Europe of the many, including Britain, to a Europe of the few, including France. More than any other state in continental Europe, the Federal Republic was exposed to, and feared, the consequences of any additional intra-European divisions that might fragment Western cohesion in the face of the Soviet threat. Furthermore, the case could be made, and it was, that Britain's membership in the European Community, welcomed by the United States, would provide an effective counterweight to France in Europe. And, finally, confidence in Germany's ability to compete successfully in the economies of scale of the Common Market was already second to none in Europe.

Although for different reasons, the French, too, still defined "Europe" as a broad organization that should include Britain. In Britain's absence the Rome Treaty would leave the French with the apprehension that had dominated the EDC debate: namely, that of being boxed into a small Europe within which France's political influence could not balance the weight of Germany's economic power. In early 1956 many believed France was insufficiently prepared for the rigors of competition in a large common market. Rather than early union, the French preferred a long period of transition, at the end of which the decision to join would be made. So deep were their misgivings about the economic and political ramifications of the Rome Treaty that even ratification by the National Assembly in 1957 did not seem irreversible. The Fourth Republic was dying, and de Gaulle, the regime's principal grave digger, did not hide his contempt for a treaty that he reportedly planned to terminate should he ever return to power.[15]

Yet, in the late 1950s, de Gaulle and Adenauer lost no time in accepting this small Europe. Not only did the Common Market work economically, but, as each leader grew increasingly comfortable with the other, personally and politically, the new arrangement offered significant advantages. Earlier, France and the Federal Republic had hoped for Britain's presence in Europe as the weight needed by each country to balance the other. Now, however, Britain's absence from the European Community confirmed both countries as Europe's co-leaders. Franco-German unity would help harmonize the European and Atlantic tunes carried by each of them respectively. French influence, barely tolerated by the United States, would be exerted through the European Community, whose machinery was already in place. Simultaneously, however, Germany's influence would be cultivated in the Atlantic community, where any deterioration of the special relationship between the United States with Britain worked to Bonn's advantage.[16] Moreover, in late 1958, a new Berlin crisis, started with a six-month Soviet ultimatum that lasted four years, confirmed France as a more reliable (meaning firmer) partner than Britain. Indeed, from 1958 to 1963, Adenauer found alarming the willingness of Prime Minister Macmillan's to negotiate the status of Berlin. In no small measure this concern relaxed the German chancellor's unease over de Gaulle's decision to veto Britain's membership in January 1963.[17]

Opposed by France and Germany, the two dominant members of the Six, Britain also failed to gain U.S. support. In 1960 the Eisenhower administration played a leading role in the creation of the Organization for Economic Cooperation and Development (OECD) as a substitute for the OEEC—the organization around which the British government had built its case against the EEC. In

1961 U.S. pressures on Britain to change course and seek admission in the Common Market increased quickly. Early concessions made by the EEC to U.S. economic interests seemed to confirm that bargaining over tariffs and other trade issues was easier with one larger European community than with two smaller ones.[18] President Kennedy hoped, as had his predecessor, that Britain's participation would steer and influence Europe at a time when de Gaulle's political challenge to U.S. leadership and policies was getting sharper and more vocal. And, finally, the recovery of Europe showed a potential for self-help and collective burden-sharing, themes that were about to become a leitmotiv of Atlantic debates. "An integrated Western Europe," Kennedy told Congress in 1962, "will further shift the world balance to the side of freedom."[19] The reasoning was the same as it had been fifteen years earlier, when President Truman had articulated his vision of Europe and the rest of the world: the containment of a powerful and aggressive Soviet Union could be best achieved with stronger and uniting allies in Europe.

U.S. pressures alone, however, did not suffice to overcome the British reluctance to join the EEC. No less significant was the fact that, beginning in January 1959, tariff-cutting in the Common Market was already moving at a pace that would permit its completion by mid-1968, eighteen months ahead of the schedule set by the Rome Treaty. As each wave of tariff cuts provided more evidence of new gains for the EEC members, Britain's skepticism about the benefits of membership faded, and its concern over the cost of abstention grew. Even before the Common Market was launched, Britain's economic performance—including production, trade, and currency movements—had fallen behind that of the EEC Six.[20] Between 1958 and 1965 trade deficits worsened steadily, amounting to an average of nearly $2 billion a year, almost double that of Italy.[21]

It would be foolish, however, to believe that beyond the case of Britain, the Rome Treaty proceeded with ease and without acrimony, from within and without alike. In the United States political enthusiasm for "Europe" overcame, but did not mute, sharp apprehensions over its consequences for the American economy.

These were exacerbated by a newly discovered problem that the countries of Europe found difficult to grasp: the deterioration of the balance of payments that Eisenhower uncovered late in his administration, and that Kennedy singled out as a threat second only to nuclear war.[22] With the renewed convertibility of the pound sterling and other leading European currencies in December 1958 causing a movement of capital away from the dollar area and back to Europe, where higher interest rates prevailed, the U.S. payments deficit exceeded $4 billion in 1959-60, compared with an average level of $1.5 billion in previous years. Faced with a dollar glut, neither the Eisenhower nor the Kennedy administration could remain indifferent to the potential rise of a high-tariff group of states in Europe that might discriminate against U.S. exporters, notwithstanding the political benefits both administrations expected from European integration.

These apprehensions were warranted. On average, the Rome Treaty set a common external tariff that was, or might be, higher than the national tariffs it was intended to replace. How this was to be achieved in spite of the restrictions imposed by the General Agreement on Tariffs and Trade (GATT) took many forms. Thus, the Rome Treaty averaged preexisting national tariffs without regard to the value of goods imported in each case. West Germany and the three Benelux countries were low-tariff countries that accounted for about two thirds of the Community's imports. Yet, since the Benelux was treated as a single unit, these four countries received the same weight as the other two high-tariff countries in the final computations, which took no account of the tariff cuts made by the German government in early 1957 because of a considerable balance-of-payments surplus with its European partners. As a result, German tariffs on most manufactured imports were doubled or more—to levels higher, in fact, than German manufacturers wanted—and the Common Market gained a protection initially higher than the average that had prevailed before the Rome Treaty.

The protectionist character of the projected market was most evident in the case of agriculture. Although the details of future arrangements were left to be worked out later, the intention of the

Rome Treaty was unmistakable: to maintain a predetermined structure of prices for agricultural commodities within each member-state while achieving nondiscriminatory treatment within the Community. Most generally, the Common Agricultural Policy (CAP) would enable EEC producers to receive a high internal support or target price. Produce that European farmers could not market at the target price were to be purchased by a CAP guarantee fund at the intervention price. Lower-priced imports were subject to variable levies and tariffs to protect domestic production. The import price or world price, combined with the levy imposed by the community, made up the threshold price. Including unloading and transportation costs the imported product was sold at the EEC target price or at the same price as the more expensively produced EEC product.[23]

The CAP would cost money, of course—even though hardly anyone anticipated how much that would be. Over the years, the cost of sustaining it grew beyond the Commission's ability to calculate (if high consumer prices as well as actual taxpayers' contributions are taken into account). Yet, given the political implications of the issue for most members of the Community, it was agreed with the French that this would be money well spent—a reasoning that has persisted even as reform programs launched every few years (in 1973, 1978, 1984, 1988, and 1991) have sought to control over-supply in order to curb budget outlays.[24] Indeed, since 1961 the fears of the Kennedy administration, which tried to scuttle the Common Agricultural Policy even before it was installed, were shown to be well-founded. EEC agricultural imports fell by one third during the ten years that followed implementation of the CAP system, even as total world agricultural imports increased by more than one half during the same period. And the form and scope of farm subsidies have remained one of the most contentious issues in intra-European and transatlantic relations.[25]

That the Six were expected to be, and became, the main benefi-ciaries of their own customs union was all too predictable. Whom else was it meant to serve? In 1958-63 intra-Community trade rose 130 percent, as compared with a general increase in world trade of 31 percent.[26] The evidence of economic gains that accompanied the acceleration of the tariff-cutting schedule and the elimination of quota restrictions was immediate. It provided for vigorous growth in industrial production, although at a slightly slower pace than was recorded during the recovery years that preceded the formation of the Common Market. In 1959-66 annual average rates of growth amounted to 5.5 percent per year in France and West Germany and 5.9 percent in Italy, as compared with 5.1, 7.6, and 4 percent for each of these three countries, respectively, in 1952-58.[27]

Such a performance helped do away with whatever lingering doubts might have remained in each member-state; hence de Gaulle's unexpected endorsement of the Common Market on May 31, 1960, as a "practical reality" that followed "the path of organizational cooperation between states while waiting to achieve, perhaps, an imposing confederation"; hence the surprising endorsement provided by the Italian Communist Party as early as 1962, when it found its earlier analysis to be "erroneous" because it had neglected the benefits that a common market would create for the Italian economy generally and its working class specifically; and hence Britain's growing anxieties about its exclusion from the EEC.[28] By the mid-1960s Britain was being projected as falling behind not only Germany but also France. By the time Britain finally entered the Common Market, it had been overtaken by all the EEC members, except Italy, even though it had been more prosperous than any of them in 1956. And, to make matters worse, by that time, too, the first phase of sustained economic expansion in the postwar industrial world was ending, thereby exacerbating the differences of national interest that had been hidden by the prosperity of the 1960s.

During the first ten years of the Common Market, trade among the Six increased by 347 percent while trade in the rest of the world rose 130 percent. By the end of that period intra-EEC trade showed a sharp rise for every one of its charter members.[29] But during this initial period at least, the trade regime put in place by the Rome Treaty did not prevent significant progress toward a more liberal Atlantic trade system: the trade deficit between the Six and the United States rose from $712 million in 1958 to about $2.5 billion in 1963. However, the recovery of Europe and Japan was already pointing to the end of the postwar era of economic unilateralism and the emergence, instead, of an economic triangle, which the Trade Expansion Act and the related Kennedy Round of tariff negotiations were designed to accommodate. In 1965 the U.S. trade surplus with Japan turned into a deficit, even though no one suspected how much it would grow in coming years; in 1968 the U.S. commercial trade surplus turned into a deficit that became nearly permanent after 1971; and in 1972 the U.S. trade surplus with Western Europe, which had proved most resilient, also turned into a deficit.[30]

Predictably, in this new international economic environment, harmony within the European Community would be more difficult to achieve, American leadership over the Atlantic community more difficult to assert, and tensions between the two more difficult to manage. But both sides of the Atlantic still remained willing to pay the price required to sustain the postwar bargain between the United States and Western Europe. There could be neither affluence nor security for either side without the other: the quest for affluence written into the European idea and the need for security written into the Atlantic idea remained complementary.

Although its negotiation was admittedly tedious and seemingly endless, the Kennedy Round was, therefore, generally successful. It satisfied the United States because it reduced the average tariffs of the six EEC states by about 50 percent and left the Common Market with fewer quantitative restrictions on a wide range of industrial products.[31] Accordingly, U.S. exporters continued to benefit from the expanding European market, as they had even before the completion of the Kennedy Round. For the full period before the enlargement of the Common Market, U.S.-EEC trade more than trebled (from $4.5 billion to $16.7 billion), after which it continued to grow faster than the average growth for world trade. The Kennedy Round also satisfied the Europeans because, even though agricultural products represented about one third of total U.S. exports to the Common Market, it preserved the elaborate CAP structure set in place in late 1961 after a French ultimatum had threatened to bring the Rome Treaty down.

Furthermore, whatever trade diversion the Common Market may have cost U.S. exporters—and hence U.S. domestic producers—was compensated for by large flows of U.S. direct investment into Europe, which increased fivefold from 1958 to 1971. Kept possible by the preserve of abundant capital and foreign exchange, rendered attractive by lower wage costs in Europe, made easier by improved communications that facilitated market access, and made desirable by fears of additional restrictions and tariffs in later years, the sharp rise in U.S. corporate investment in Europe overshadowed in economic and political significance the decline of exports to the Continent. The number of U.S. affiliates in the EEC, which had grown by 2.9 percent a year in 1950-57, grew at a yearly average of 14.3 percent during the decade that followed the Rome Treaty.[32] Nor was U.S. corporate interest denied. Instead, it was sought actively by most EEC countries, which offered all sorts of concessions that helped maximize profits. At the end of 1957, the last pre-Common Market year, the total book value of American direct investment in the six EEC countries stood at 6.6 percent of all U.S. direct investment abroad. It amounted to 12.7 percent in 1965, and it reached 14.9 percent by 1970, thereby making U.S. firms in Europe the dominant, and in some leading sectors the only, true "European" giants.[33]

In sum, while the Atlantic security community continued to serve Europe's political interests well, an expanding European Economic Community also served U.S. economic interests well. Thirty years after the signing of the Rome Treaty, which, it was feared, would be an obstacle to the growth of commercial relations with Europe, the twelve members of the European Community bought 24 percent of U.S. exports, more than Canada and twice as much as Japan. The U.S. share of direct investment in the EC had grown to nearly 40 percent, and the sale of U.S.-owned affiliates in the Community came to $620 billion, compared with $29 billion in 1960. All told, America and Europe now engage in nearly one trillion dollars worth of transactions each year.[34]

Europe des Nations?

"Europe" could hardly be limited to a customs union, whether that of the privileged Six gathered in a small Common Market, or that of seven of the other European countries that Britain grouped, *faute de mieux*, into a free trade association (EFTA) in January 1960. To proceed toward the "ever closer union" evoked by the Rome Treaty, the EEC countries needed to explore and develop other dimensions for the Community. Drawing on the logic of the European Defense Community, an elaborate draft for political union had been proposed in March 1953: obviously, there could not be a common army without common political institutions that would deal with matters of foreign policy. Linked to the EDC, that proposal died with it in 1954. For the French Fourth Republic, one dose of supranationalism, already swallowed with the European Coal and Steel Community, was the most that could be accepted in one generation. Even under duress, more was too much. For Britain, even one-half dose was too much.[35]

In the 1950s Britain's wavering was a significant feature of France's dismissal of a design that sought to build a European political identity that would strengthen the Atlantic personality shaped a few years earlier. In the 1960s, however, the reverse proved to be true. According to de Gaulle's France, extending the Community to political matters demanded a habit of cooperation that would be distinct from, though not necessarily in opposition to, the integrated practices followed in NATO. Even though Britain shared de Gaulle's concept of a *Europe des nations* that respected the primacy of the nation-state, it represented, therefore, a threat to the European identity envisioned by the French president so long as its ties with the United States were not explicitly curtailed. Pending a tangible demonstration of Britain's European good faith, which de Gaulle sought in the area of nuclear cooperation in late 1962, political union in Europe, modestly outlined in terms of meetings strictly limited by the right of national veto, would have to be undertaken without, and even against, Britain. In essence, this is what the French proposed to do in 1961 with a plan that carried the name of Christian Fouchet, the first chairman of the committee that drafted it.[36]

But even without Britain in the Community, de Gaulle feared the influence that the United States might have on the smaller EEC states, especially Holland, Britain's close ally on the Continent. Accordingly, in 1965, when Walter Hallstein, the first president of the European Commission, proposed a reform of the Rome Treaty that would give the Commission new authority to initiate action on some matters against the opposition of two thirds of the EEC members, the Community was faced with one of its most difficult and enduring crises. In early 1962 de Gaulle's own revisions of the Fouchet Plan had gone precisely in the opposite direction: to reduce the autonomous power of the Commission by including economic affairs in the purview of the heads of government.[37] Now, Hallstein appeared to bypass the French veto by making it possible for, say, Belgium and Luxemburg, to act against the will of their partners. With the benign approval of Chancellor Ludwig Erhard—less tolerant of de Gaulle and more favorable to Britain than his predecessor—Hallstein, de Gaulle bitterly complained, was trying to move Europe toward a federation whose agent and federator would be implicitly the Federal Republic. He was, the French president later wrote derisively, just "a German ambitious for his country."[38]

De Gaulle's opposition to Britain's entry in the Common Market in 1963, which was debated for another ten years; his imposition of the Luxemburg compromise of January 1966, which gave member-states an unqualified right to veto Community decisions and lasted for another twenty years; and his withdrawal from NATO a few months later, which remained a part of the French political consensus for the rest of the Cold War, all formed a whole that postponed indefinitely any truly new political initiative about "Europe" until the 1987 Single European Act. After de Gaulle's resignation, to be sure, the principles that had guided the Fouchet proposals were resurrected by President Pompidou at the Hague summit of December 1969. But the process of European Political Cooperation (EPC) that began in the fall of 1970 remained structurally loose, predictably timid, and substantively vague even as Europe—known as the European

Communities (EC) after 1965, when the ECSC, the EEC, and Euratom were merged into one community—doubled its membership from six to twelve members.

Before the EC's enlargement in 1973, any such procedure for "better mutual comprehension" among its member-states added little to the bilateral consultative framework organized by de Gaulle and Adenauer in 1963; with the EPC denied the treaty status that might have provided it with at least the semblance of formal authority, it could hardly be conducive to any sort of joint action. After 1973, the issues over which de Gaulle had waged battle against France's partners in the Community were taken up by Britain: the size and composition of the Community's budget, which was challenged by Prime Ministers Harold Wilson and James Callaghan for the balance of the 1970s, and the role and power of the Commission relative to those of the Council, which was a main feature of Prime Minister Margaret Thatcher's opposition to Europe throughout the 1980s.

After de Gaulle, France's objections to Britain's entry in the Community ended, mostly to facilitate a monetary *relance* that would protect Europe against the currency crises that began in 1967 after years of unusual stability. By then, of course, Britain's determination to enter the Common Market could no longer be questioned, unlike what had been the case in 1961, when its bid had remained ambivalent. Continued exclusion, it was now feared, would inflict significant pain on Britain's economy. Moreover, Germany's growing influence in the Community revived the French interest in a counterweight that would be best provided by Britain. Finally, acquiescence to Britain's bid might help the French government gain Germany's support for a monetary scheme that would move Europe closer to the fixed exchange rates it favored. In any case, the Economic and Monetary Union (EMU) that the Six agreed to seek in December 1969 was expected to give them "a common international monetary personality" that would shield them from the dollar at a time when the U.S. payments deficit was rising at an unprecedented pace: the combined total of all U.S. deficits for the whole decade of the 1960s ($10.43 billion) was nearly equaled in 1970 ($10.25 billion), and nearly trebled in 1971 ($28.71 billion).

Admittedly, the EMU was a momentous undertaking.[39] Implemented in full, the plan that outlined it—given the name of one of its main architects, Pierre Werner—might have caused an unprecedented transfer of national sovereignty in the budgetary and monetary fields. Proposed at a time when military force appeared to be devalued as the main currency of power, its potential impact on Europe might have been equal to that of the European Defense Community twenty years earlier. Its timing could not have been worse, however. In 1971-73 the dollar float created an exchange rate volatility that European currencies could neither escape nor contain. In 1973 the first oil crisis worsened balance-of-payments problems and rising inflation and dealt a terminal blow to a system that, by its very nature, needed more, and not less, stability.

The first three-year stage of the Werner Plan that was adopted in early 1971 was designed to narrow the margin of fluctuation among EC currencies. A few months after the Nixon administration ended the convertibility of the dollar in August 1971, the monetary coordination envisioned by the Six in the Basle agreement of April 1972 sought to contain currency fluctuation within a common band of 2.25 percent (the "snake") oscillating within the wider band (the "tunnel") allowed under the Smithsonian agreement of December 1971—but that was not enough. When the dollar was allowed to float freely in March 1973, the tunnel was abandoned—but too late. Even as the European monetary authorities pretended that they could maintain a zone of relative monetary stability defined by a joint float against the U.S. currency, the oil crisis later that year left the snake unable to withstand the new economic and monetary instabilities that followed. As the Werner Plan had made few provisions for credit to countries with balance-of-payments difficulties, the snake gave way to a truncated exchange rate arrangement centered on the deutsche mark and limited to two non-EC countries, Norway and Sweden, in addition to the Benelux countries.

As with the EDC in 1954, failure of the EMU left "Europe" astray amidst apparently irreconcilable intra-European differences over economic policies (especially between inflation-prone France and inflation-shy Germany), political aspirations (exacerbated by the difficult circumstances under which Britain entered the Common Market), and institutional quarrels (over the status and influence of the Commission's swelling bureaucratic apparatus in Brussels). In late 1973 the political *sauve-qui-peut* that accompanied the oil embargo exposed Europe's submission to emerging global challenges that the nine EEC members could address neither collectively nor individually: the ascendancy of Japan's economic power combined with the emergence of other new industrial competitors in Asia; the rise of Soviet military power and ambitions combined with an apparent devaluation of American power and will; and growing instabilities in the Third World, where Europe's interest in raw materials and markets remained vital. Even as the European continent was literally running out of gas, the idea of Europe appeared to be running out of time.[40]

Europe's decline seemed even more irreversible after Chancellor Brandt's replacement by Helmut Schmidt in May 1974 threatened to upset the Franco-German partnership.[41] Although Willy Brandt hardly achieved with Pompidou the kind of relationship developed between de Gaulle and Adenauer, he had reversed the conflictual trends inherited from his two predecessors, Ludwig Erhard in 1963-66 and, to a lesser extent, Kurt Kiesinger in 1966-69. Not only did Pompidou and Brandt manage to accommodate their differences in, and on behalf of, Europe, they also formed a surprisingly cordial relationship with their counterpart in London, Edward Heath, whose first priority as prime minister was to negotiate the terms of Britain's entry in the Community.

By 1974 Germany's commitment to European unity could no longer be taken for granted. To a visceral distrust of the Commission in Brussels, which was shared by most of Schmidt's partners, added an increasingly vocal exasperation with Europe's reliance on Germany as its "paymaster"—whether for the Common Agricultural Policy or for regional aid, both increasingly costly. And a natural penchant for assertiveness predisposed the new German chancellor to challenge the leadership of France's new president, Valéry Giscard d'Estaing, a man who shared so many of Schmidt's personal traits as to make a Franco-German clash for the leadership of Europe at least very likely if not inevitable.

Such was not to be, however; instead, both men soon displayed a compatibility that strengthened the Franco-German entente and served as the basis for a new *relance* of Europe. The ties between Schmidt and Giscard differed fundamentally from those that had united de Gaulle and Adenauer. Then, the intimacy between these two aging statesmen had been rooted mostly in a shared history, which also produced the deep suspicion that each man showed toward the other's country. Never mind de Gaulle's affection for Adenauer. When the French president sought a *directoire* with Britain and the United States in 1958, it was without, and even against, Germany. Neither Eisenhower nor Kennedy showed much interest in an initiative that was too obviously aimed at one of the key members of the Western Alliance. Never mind the Franco-German Treaty of Friendship and Cooperation. When de Gaulle sought a broader *directoire* in 1969—this time without the United States—it was on the basis of Anglo-French bilateral negotiations that de Gaulle hoped to keep secret from the Federal Republic (as well as from the fourth projected member, Italy). The Foreign Office in London lost little time in making the French intentions known in Bonn and elsewhere, which would probably have postponed Britain's entry in the Community indefinitely had not de Gaulle resigned a few months later.

The history Giscard and Schmidt had lived was not that of World War II but of the Cold War. Accordingly, the fear they felt most was rooted less in shared memories of the past than in a common vision of the future—in the vision of a Europe that refused to remain forever dependent on the interplay of American and Soviet power. The weak political base both men held after their respective elections in May 1974, a few days apart, was amply compensated by an arrogance that might have been expected in Paris but that, in Bonn, showed that the impact of defeat was beginning to fade and a new political confidence was beginning to emerge.

Giscard and Schmidt liked each other. Better yet, after they had both served as finance ministers, and after they had both moved on to their new responsibilities, they understood and even admired each other. Together they launched the European Council in December

1974 to replace the more formal European summits arranged by Pompidou and Brandt. In effect, they were resurrecting the yearly meetings of EC heads of government that had been proposed by the Fouchet Plan. As Jean Monnet put it, these meetings would now serve to organize decisions, mostly managed *à deux*, rather than to manage discussions, always organized with all members.[42] Together Schmidt and Giscard co-presided over these meetings as if they were cabinet meetings, and issues of vital interest to all members were debated before being taken up by the Commission, whose president, Roy Jenkins, the two men also selected together in 1977.

Notwithstanding their regal outlook on their respective domestic environments, they proposed, also jointly, that the European Parliament be elected through direct elections—which took place in 1979, perhaps as a first step toward the direct election of a European president, which Giscard hoped to become after his election to a second seven-year term as France's president (an election that, of course, he lost in 1981). Notwithstanding their doubts over the benefits of Britain's membership in the Community, the two men agreed to the renegotiation of its terms of entry, which their respective successors were to conclude at the 1984 summit in Fontainebleau. And notwithstanding their awareness of the broad divergences between their respective economies, they proposed, in 1978, a new European Monetary System (EMS), which became operational in March 1979, without the inflated rhetoric and excessive goals of the Pompidou-Brandt initiative for economic and monetary union ten years earlier.

Money and the Price of Unity

The price of economic and monetary union is high. Binding rules alone do not suffice to make what is economically desirable in one country acceptable for its partners. Monetary and fiscal discipline causes economic pain that exacts much political cost as well. Thus, the coordination of economic policies also requires a large measure of suasion. Separated by national boundaries, electorates cannot be coordinated, even for the election of European parliamentarians, whose selection continues to respond to national rather than European issues. Voters in each country define priorities to which their governments remain predictably sensitive. Accordingly, countries that monetary union might affect adversely, in terms of unemployment, price stability, or growth, may feel a need to resort to policies that tend to undermine the system's cohesiveness. This need may prove especially compelling in the absence of adequate provisions for a steady transfer of resources from the economically strong and politically satisfied to the economically weak and politically unstable. In short, community makes monetary union possible, but monetary union does not make a community.

Like most other decisions about Europe, the EMS was a political decision whose price, admittedly uncertain, was preferable to the cost of doing nothing. In the late 1970s parallel events in currency, gold, oil, and capital markets threatened the economic health of all EC member-states, and, therefore, the political health of their respective governing majorities (most of which were, in fact, to be voted out of office in the first few years of the system).[43] Doing nothing meant continued reliance on America's ability to manage these disorders. Yet the failure of U.S.-Soviet détente, as well as the conditions that surrounded the end of the war in Vietnam and the beginning of the first oil crisis, inspired little confidence in the solutions proposed by the United States for dealing with turbulence. Doing something was not without risk either. In the Community the *Bundesbank* had ample reasons to warn Schmidt not to trust his EC partners, especially France: five years and three devaluations of the French franc later, withdrawal from the EMS was seriously considered by the first government of a newly elected socialist government in Paris. But Schmidt trusted Giscard's political commitment to Europe more readily than he believed the *Bundesbank*'s economic warnings against the EMS.

In practice, the EMS relied on economic suasion as its governing principle. Membership was offered *à la carte*. EC countries could join the system in toto, or they could choose to stay out of its most burdensome feature, the Exchange Rate Mechanism (ERM). Unlike the Bretton Woods regime, which had imposed only one narrow margin of fluctuation of plus or minus 1 percent, the ERM made allowance for two broader margins: plus or minus 2.25 percent and plus or minus 6 percent (the latter of which was adopted by Italy in 1979, all new EC members in the 1980s, and Britain after it joined the ERM in 1990). The aim of the entire system was not to lock in currencies at specific and rigid levels of exchange rates; it was, instead, to limit the frequency and the size of any adjustments. Responsibility for making exchange rate adjustments was left up to national authorities. Should imbalances persist, the system also made room for a greater and easier allocation of automatic credits (more than double what the Werner Plan had proposed) and for a larger and more effective program of regional development.

At first, prospects for the EMS looked no better than the stillborn Werner Plan. Since the economic circumstances that made a political *relance* necessary also made its implementation difficult, economists usually dismissed it, and politicians often ignored it. To many, a simpler arrangement against the dollar would have been preferable. Giscard and Schmidt, however, feared that any such arrangement would work to the advantage of the Commission, whose influence they meant to reduce, or at least contain, but certainly not enhance.[44] The complexity of the system, including the range of the target zones, left it highly vulnerable to destabilizing speculative capital movements, as financial markets anticipated and then precipitated frequent—and, given the agreed bands of fluctuation, even sizable—exchange rate adjustments. The markets were not wrong, despite the many exchange controls kept in place throughout the 1980s, and still allowed in the early 1990s, as a temporary escape from the rigors of the liberalization of capital movements. By the end of 1990 exchange rate variability still averaged about 0.7 percent a month for all ERM countries.[45]

Although the EMS did not preclude some exchange rate changes, there had to be a limit to their frequency; otherwise, the new monetary regime would lose the significance it was intended to have.[46] These limits, though, did not emerge readily. Strong demand for the deutsche mark pushed its rate up, not only against the dollar in September 1979 but also against most other EMS currencies in

October 1981, June 1982, and March 1983. At best, the system seemed irrelevant. Between 1979 and 1983, high, higher, and highly different rates of inflation and budget deficits forced difficult currency realignments.[47] Nor, finally, was there much interest in a European currency, the Ecu, which, as a fixed basket of European currencies, was heralded as a central feature of the system but remained widely ignored by most European firms as their best hedge against currency instabilities.[48]

Yet, despite this difficult start, the EMS performed well in the stormy international monetary markets that accompanied the fall of the dollar after February 1985, when the dollar's peak prompted the general EMS currency realignment of July 1985.[49] After that, the system began to provide for unexpected stability in the European money markets, as its members recognized that forcing a surplus country to a price level closer to the Community's average in the name of exchange rate stability was more undesirable, politically and in other terms, than the reverse.[50] There was no currency adjustment from January 1987 to January 1990. With the rate mechanism enforced by the EMS encouraging governments to keep money fairly tight in order to maintain their currency high in the upper half of its band, inflation rates were driven down toward the rate of the lowest-inflation country—West Germany—thereby causing a significant reduction of inflation differentials within the whole system.

After the currency realignment of March 1983, especially, the annual rate of inflation in the Federal Republic, which averaged slightly more than 2 percent in the 1980s (and less than 1.5 percent during the second half of the decade), became the target rate of the whole system. During the first years of the EMS, inflation had grown higher and faster within the EMS than in other industrial countries; after 1985, it fell lower and faster. By mid-1989 the eight full members of the EMS, *cum* the ERM, had an average inflation rate of 3.5 percent, ranging from Holland's 1 percent to Italy's 6.75 percent. The four outsiders—Britain, Greece, Portugal, and Spain—had an average rate of 10.75 percent.

With the deutsche mark thus emerging as a de facto anchor against inflation, high-inflation countries pursued counterinflationary policies that demonstrated their acceptance of, and conversion to, the rigor of the system, thereby permitting the measure of economic convergence that had been missing in the original conception of the system in 1979. Interest rate differentials in the EMS, another key indicator of economic convergence, also narrowed. Even before Germany's unification began to have an impact on its rates, there remained no practical difference between interest rates in Germany and the Netherlands, and the difference between France and Belgium was negligible.

Thus, inflation-prone countries borrowed credibility from West Germany, whose historical commitment to price stability in turn served to reduce inflationary expectations, even though the German government never set an irrevocably fixed target. In return, intra-EMS bilateral exchange rate stability served to moderate, and in some cases void, the impact that a fluctuating U.S. dollar had on the deutsche mark vis-à-vis other EMS currencies: namely, to weaken when the dollar gained strength, and to gain strength when the dollar weakened. Thus, as Germany's trade surplus with the United States fell from 28 billion deutsche marks in 1986 to 17 billion in 1988, its surplus with other EMS members rose from 30 to 46 billion deutsche marks, almost eight times the 1983 figure.[51] And the EC share of the Federal Republic's global trade surplus rose from 53.8 percent for the first quarter 1987 to 65.9 percent for the same period in 1988. This was a convincing payoff for the transformation of the EMS into an increasingly asymmetrical monetary system, with the West German currency at its center and the other currencies at the periphery.

As currencies stabilized, however, economic growth also slowed, amounting to 2.9 percent for EMS members (for the years 1985-89) as compared with 3.6 percent for European states that did not participate in the EMS and its ERM. This exercise in collective austerity proved quite painful for many of its members. But the political will to accept such pain also made it possible to turn away from established national practices. In France a socialist government allowed real wages to rise by less than 6 percent between 1983 and 1989, but in Britain a conservative government allowed real wage increases of 20 percent during the same period. Lower rates of economic growth caused higher rates of unemployment, which necessitated a politically difficult reordering of domestic priorities. In Britain, where the economy grew two times faster than in France from 1983 to 1987, Prime Minister Thatcher continued to overwhelm her political opposition; in France President Mitterrand lost the legislative elections of May 1987 after unemployment rose to 10.5 percent (as compared with 7.4 percent in 1981). Although unemployment peaked in most EMS countries by 1987, or shortly thereafter, it remained markedly higher than in the United States and other OECD countries in subsequent years.[52] As a pointed reminder of the price of monetary union, during the six months that followed Britain's entry in the ERM in late 1990, its rate of inflation was reduced by nearly half, but at the cost of a recession that was deeper than that of any other major industrial country over the same period.

In all instances the political risk was assumed when references to "Europe" served to justify economic policies that might not have been justifiable on other grounds. In Italy exchange rate discipline denied traditionally weak governments the political comfort of devaluations, which, throughout the 1970s, had allowed industry to offset excessive pay raises and cost increases. In the mid-1980s the wage indexing system known as *la scala mobile* was weakened at last, and industry improved productivity by restructuring and investing in new technologies. In January 1990 the realignment of the lira—the first in the EMS in three years—came together with Italy's acceptance of the narrow 2.25 percent fluctuation band, instead of the wider 6 percent band it had adopted since 1979. In France the fight against inflation ceased to be the focus of partisan political debates and, as of the fall of 1987, helped the economy perform at a pace that surpassed expectations, at least until the slowdown of 1990-91. A strong and stable franc, and an unprecedented rise in investment, also improved France's competitive position in the single market, for which the French began to prepare earlier and more aggressively than their EC partners. In Spain, where notoriously low productivity had been traditionally offset by low wages and layers of unabashed protectionism, Felipe González opened the country's industry to the competitive pressures of the

Common Market first, and to the monetary rigor of the ERM next. In April 1991 Madrid's decision to lift its last remaining controls on capital outflows well ahead of the agreed deadline had no effect on the Spanish currency.

Even before the Revolutions of 1989 carried Europe past the Cold War and its divisions, therefore, "Europe" was going through its most significant achievement since the launching of the Common Market in 1957. In this sense the political will revealed to make the EMS work unveiled a Community that challenged the sovereignty of the nation-state over the vital issue of money. In 1987 the Single European Act broadened this challenge further. The issue raised by the act was not only the organization of a single economic market by 1992, which had already been anticipated nearly three decades earlier. No less, and perhaps more, significantly, the SEA exorcised the taboo that had prevented consideration of any change in the Rome Treaty: by making a few elementary institutional reforms possible, the act created a credible precedent for new and even more ambitious reforms in the future.[53]

As we have seen, the EMS first emphasized the relatively limited goals of reducing the volatility of exchange rates, minimizing currency realignments, and reducing key economic divergences in the direction of the best-performing member of the system. But no single market *à l'américaine* could prosper with fragmented political institutions *à l'européenne*. The monetary *relance* of 1979, written into the EMS, and the economic *relance* of 1987, written into the SEA, converged most logically in the 1989 proposal for a fully fixed or single currency system explicitly committed to price stability and including an independent European central bank above the national central banks.

But why change a system that was proving as effective as the EMS? The mere anticipation of a community-wide agreement on the EMU might generate inflationary expectations, as the new central bank would be forced to earn its anti-inflationary reputation, which the *Bundesbank* has inherited from Germany's history. Now at issue, therefore, is whether any such European central bank—which, however it might be designed and governed would be more open to political influence than the *Bundesbank*-led ERM—could gain and would maintain the same anti-inflationary credibility as Germany's central bank.

In the 1960s the Bretton Woods system, too, was a hegemonic system that appeared to be creating the conditions for a unified currency zone—the dollar area. Inflation rates had converged at a very low level, which was mostly determined by the pace of world money growth.[54] In this instance, however, economic growth was not sacrificed. On the contrary, growth remained robust throughout the OECD countries, especially for those regions, and for the countries within each region, that needed it most: Europe (and Japan) relative to the United States, for example, or Portugal and Greece relative to Europe. Yet, within a few years, the U.S. anchor lost the ballast it needed to keep the system aright, and no country or group of countries could step up to take its place. Inflation in the United States, which had remained well below the average rate of inflation in other OECD countries every year from 1961 through 1966, exceeded that average from 1967 through 1970. The U.S. payments deficit, which had averaged $1 billion per year during the previous ten years, rose to more than $18 billion per year in 1970-72. The excess of international reserves could not be sterilized by surplus countries that were politically sensitive to the consequences of the required deflationary policies. World inflation was thus well on its way before the 1973 oil crisis.

In the absence of any built-in device that can guarantee the stability of the system, or permit a return to stability in case of external shocks, a hegemonic monetary system *à la* EMS that relies on a national currency as a parallel currency is intrinsically fragile.[55] In effect, it is at the mercy of one country's ability to act, and to continue to act, as a central reserve currency country on behalf of partners that are, and remain, willing to subordinate policies accordingly. Unless it is strengthened when it appears to be working best, such a system is bound to collapse sooner or later.[56]

The experience of the Bretton Woods system is all the more relevant to the EMS, as, unlike the United States, Germany, even unified, is not a sufficiently large country relative to its partners in

Europe and its economy is more vulnerable to external shocks than was the U.S. economy. In addition, because Germany's market faces competition from London and possibly Paris, the deutsche mark's primacy is not as complete as the dollar's was during the first twenty years of the Bretton Woods system. In 1979-83 political changes throughout the EC countries gave the EMS a new lease on life and monetary stability. This lease could be terminated just as easily as it was extended with the series of European elections scheduled for the period 1992-95. What would be, say, the policy of a Labor-led government in Britain? Or how will the battle over Mitterrand's succession in 1995 or before shape France's economic policy? And, even more compellingly, can Germany itself remain reliable as it confronts the economic burden of unification? Or will the German anchor give way just as, in earlier years, the Vietnam War loosened up the American anchor and left the Bretton Woods system adrift?

As envisioned by Jacques Delors, the Commission's president, the EMU would necessarily cause a transfer of monetary policy from the member-states to the Community. At once or in due time, a European central bank would become operationally independent of national governments—no less, and possibly more than, the *Bundesbank*, since it would not be accountable to a strong and coherent political authority. Even more contentiously, the EMU might also necessitate a significant transfer of fiscal policy as well, especially in the politically sensitive area of budgetary discipline (for which some EC members already seek binding rules and sanctions). Not surprisingly, such prospects are sources of apprehension for countries that wish to avoid diluting their sovereignty any more than they already have.

Once again, however, a step in the direction of European integration is leading to further initiatives in other directions. In 1985 the EMS had already become what it was not expected to be, as the *Bundesbank* gained an influence that went beyond what initially had been foreseen. In 1987 agreement on the organization of a single market for the twelve members of the European Community strengthened a compelling logic leading to a subsequent agreement on economic and monetary union. And in turn, the logic of economic and monetary union has implied a European political union, which President Mitterrand and Chancellor Kohl recognized in their joint appeal of April 1990. To be sure, nothing in this process is either automatic or inevitable. But at this stage of Europe's journey, and given what has been unveiled of the European Community, a multispeed EMU offered to the EC states *à la carte*, as was the case with EMS and as has been the case with nearly everything else, has already become irreversible. The process has moved too far to be delayed too long, and the journey has proceeded far too long to avoid moving further.

Wanted: A Single Voice

The discipline achieved over issues of trade and money cannot be found in the political arena yet. Even the modest and informal procedures for European political consultation outlined by the Davignon Committee in October 1970 were left to an informal consultative body that lacked both formal power and incentives to bring its members to some agreement on a common foreign policy or on any revision of the Rome Treaties (until the proposal for the Single European Act). If anything, when facing one of the many international crises that characterized the last twenty years of the Cold War, each member-state used self-serving references to "Europe" as a cover for doing less, or nothing, in order to offend no one. Diluting any action, or explaining inaction, in the name of the necessity for, or commitment to, European solidarity remained a way of life for "Europe."[57] If anything, its calls for solidarity provided mostly a convenient shelter from a U.S. leadership questioned by some of its members on any one issue, rather than the active, credible, and responsible mechanism needed by all of them to protect their common interests. No less, and perhaps more, than any other factor, Europe's passivity on anything other than the predictable criticism of U.S. policies contributed to the rise of "Europessimism" in the 1970s.

During and after the first oil crisis, the countries of Western Europe behaved, therefore, mostly as hecklers on the world stage. In a series of international crises involving some of their most vital interests, their collective role, if any, appeared limited to taunting an American leadership that was feared for what it did as much as for what it failed to do. Not only in the Middle East and the Gulf, but also, later, vis-à-vis the Soviet Union and over regional issues from southern Africa to Southwest Asia, Europeans seemed to raise their voices only to carp and complain. Conversely, in the United States, intra-European divisions in the face of these crises, as well as occasional displays of unified European opposition, served only to increase Americans' alienation from allies whose recovery had failed to reduce, and might even have worsened, the security burdens assumed on their behalf after the war. In short, whether it spoke aloud or said nothing, the European voice introduced a tone of discord in transatlantic relations. Regarding the military threat in the East especially, little was heard that might have made it worth listening to; regarding the economic threat in the Third World, little was said that was pleasant to hear. Growing transatlantic rivalry caused by an increasingly assertive European Community in the areas of trade and money, and growing transatlantic discord caused by a continuously benign (and occasionally malign) Community in the areas of foreign and defense policy, appeared to threaten the future of both Europe and its ties with the United States.

The distinction between the passivity of European countries in Europe, which involved the fact of Soviet power and the risk of U.S.-Soviet confrontation, and their activism in the Third World, where the dangers raised by any such confrontation were thought to be more limited, is significant. Initially, the countries of Europe construed the European idea as a substitute for the Atlantic idea. Indeed, they began to translate the European idea into a Community (ECSC, EEC, EC) even before they accepted its implication (a diminished sovereignty of the nation-state) should the idea become a reality. Conversely, they accepted the Atlantic idea as a necessity (the Atlantic Alliance) even before they began to develop it as a reality (NATO). The European Community was expected to help provide its members with prosperity; over Germany especially, it had a security dimension that aimed at ending the threat of war from within. The Atlantic community was expected to provide security from external aggression; thanks especially to the United States, it also had a political dimension that was explicitly written into the North Atlantic Treaty (Article 2). Yet, given the issues addressed primarily within each setting, the Atlantic voice that responded to the security issues raised by the Cold War often muted the European voice that responded to other political and economic issues raised outside of the Cold War context—that is, mostly but not exclusively, in the Third World.[58]

This distinction between the NATO area and the out-of-area regions of the Third World did not result from the Cold War alone, when, admittedly, Soviet military power in Europe could be contained only by the countervailing presence of American power. Even before the end of World War II, the American liberal tradition had begun to clash with the European colonial legacy. As suggested earlier, the postwar loss of empires reduced many of the countries of Western Europe to feeble territorial skeletons that later attempted to regain the physical bulk they needed through the European Community. It was from there, in Brussels and in their lost territories of the South, that the EC states could best regain, collectively and at a small cost, the imperial vocation they had lived previously as nation-states.

Thus, the Lomé agreements, first signed in 1975, provided an early demonstration of the EC's predilection for protected markets with the former colonies of its member-states, in Africa (and in the Pacific and the Caribbean), over the open and global economy favored by the United States. In the Middle East and in the Gulf, Europe's energy dependence drove a wedge between the Community's quest for an autonomous Euro-Arab policy and the U.S. insistence on a Western consensus to achieve peace and stability in this region—not to mention stability of oil supplies at an acceptable price. With respect to Latin America and the Caribbean, domestic political concerns prompted widespread criticism of U.S. policies in most EC countries, with the exception of Britain. In sum, everywhere in the Third World the EC states have found it easier to speak with a European voice than with a collective Atlantic voice because nearly everywhere in these regions a European interest shaped by the memories of history and the realities of geography has remained more tangible than an Atlantic interest defined by the rhetoric of the Cold War and a shared commitment to common values.

That such a trend appeared to peak during the latter years of the Carter administration should come as no surprise. By then EC countries found that the U.S. protection, to which they had become accustomed since the end of World War II, had been eroded by the Soviet will to use its rising military power and by American unwillingness to use its own military power. By then, too, they increasingly feared the U.S. potential for harming their vital economic interests, especially, but not exclusively, in the Middle East and the Persian Gulf. Thus, the voice that emerged out of the tedious process of European Political Cooperation that unfolded in the 1970s seemed more directly concerned with the American threat to the economic security of Europe than with the Soviet threat to its physical security.

In the 1980s, however, the EPC adopted a more constructive tone—not always set in reaction to the United States—and, on occasion, displayed more substance too. Europe's emerging posture reflected concern over a renewed escalation in Cold War tensions, which caused a parallel improvement in Atlantic relations more than it pointed to an improvement in the EC's foreign policy collective machinery. After Carter, the European allies still found much to deplore about America's unilateralism, including, at first, the form and objectives of Reagan's policies toward the Soviet Union. Yet evidence of Soviet military ascendancy and global ambitions created a challenge that could no longer be ignored, in Europe and else- where. And, given the priority the Reagan administration gave that challenge, it, too, reduced the demands on Atlantic cohesion to a more selective and more manageable range of issues—as, for example, it complained less of transatlantic differences over North-South political issues or West-West economic issues that were deemed of lesser significance than East-West security issues.

These differences soon narrowed. Over security issues in Europe, the Reagan administration transformed the contentious issue of U.S. intermediate-range nuclear force deployment into the most impressive display of Atlantic and intra-European cohesion in two decades. Later, during the final phase of the war between Iran and Iraq, effective coordination was achieved between the United States and five of the seven members of the Western European Union in clearing mines from the Persian Gulf. In both instances, which involved vital interests for both Europe and the United States, the lesson was the same. Security interests among the members of the European Community could converge without there being divergence of interests between the Community and the United States. This lesson, which should have been all too obvious and yet had remained all too obscure, was confirmed soon afterward, in the same region, the Gulf, but under the changed conditions of the end of the Cold War and the absence of Soviet power.

In 1987 the adoption of the Single European Act (SEA) marked the most significant *relance européenne* since the Rome Treaty three decades earlier. The SEA, however, was not meant to carry, directly or indirectly, a single tone aimed, in any one area, at drowning out the American voice. On the contrary, it was motivated by a renewed urge to emulate an American model that had regained its political and economic appeal at a time when Europe was most troubled by its own economic performance (especially in the areas of job creation and competitiveness) and political irrelevance (especially in the East, but also in the Middle East). As the Reagan administration managed the country's economic expansion at home, and as it demonstrated renewed political self-confidence abroad, the American model was rendered even more attractive among the new socialist majorities in southern Europe, whose alternative programs, which had been faithfully nurtured during the many years of opposition, failed miserably and quickly.

To this extent, coming before the Revolutions of 1989 in Eastern Europe, the push toward European unity written into the Single European Act had little to do with a "decline" of American power in the face of the Soviet challenge, as might have been the case during the previous decade.[59] Instead, coming together with Mikhail Gorbachev's emphatic acknowledgment of Soviet failures at home and abroad, such U.S.-inspired renewal of "Europe" already confirmed that the Cold War was ending on American terms—namely, those outlined by the Truman administration forty years earlier, including a strong and united Western Europe, a liberated central and Eastern Europe, and a reunited but aligned German state.

In the first few crises that followed the end of the Cold War, the Community's voice could be heard, therefore, with an American accent that had been missing since the first few crises that accompanied the beginning of the Cold War. The quick reaction to the revolutions in Eastern Europe, in unison with U.S. calls for the EC's leading role in the reconstruction of the former Soviet allies, and the unprecedented exercise in collective security that countered Iraq's invasion of Kuwait in August 1990 are cases in point. To be sure, the devaluation of Soviet power might easily explain both. Yet, to repeat, no less significant was the accommodation of intra-European and transatlantic differences that preceded these new conditions in the Soviet Union, the logical outcome of which was the unity shown in 1989-91.

In the Gulf, especially, the willingness shown by France and Britain, as well as most other EC countries, to join the United States in an action that might involve the use of force confirmed how much "Europe" had overcome the divisiveness that had accompanied events in Iran ten years earlier and war in the Middle East nearly twenty years before. In August 1990 the Community's quick imposition of comprehensive sanctions against Iraq demonstrated an ability to act urgently if not decisively. Now, too, the EC states' reliance on the WEU as the vehicle for taking action, including the naval contributions of Belgium, Italy, and Spain to the embargo, suggested an ability to take collective action on behalf of shared interests without provoking new differences with the United States. In sum, since the end of the Cold War, defining Europe has ceased to be a question of defining it against either one of the two superpowers—neither against the Soviet Union nor against the United States, but with both of them.

4
Defining Europe

E urope need not, and cannot, mean the disappearance of the nations that compose it. Deeply rooted in a storied past that is recounted and celebrated from the earliest age, the nation-state still maintains an unparalleled capacity to inspire loyalty and obedience. No mere political institution, the state embraces and, almost literally, defines a community, endows it or condemns it with a history, and, over time, instills in it a collective identity and purpose. A single market can hardly inspire comparable emotions or the same sense of commitment. The citizens of Europe will always be Germans, Danes, or Italians, whose languages they will continue to use, and whose attitudes they will continue to display, as natives, even as their children absorb other languages and adopt other attitudes from the broader European community to which they have been learning to belong.

"Europe" is a creation of the mind more than it is a creation of the heart. It is not sought as a matter of choice between ideals but is accepted as a matter of necessity in the face of a narrowing range of unsatisfactory alternatives. Being simply French or Belgian or Dutch has ceased to be sufficient. The need to be "somebody" or part of "something" else is an intrinsic part of the European vision, a need that Jean Monnet, certainly the most legitimate of the many fathers of Europe, was especially eager to emphasize. But Monnet's vision was not limited to Europe alone: "Europe," he hoped, would contribute to the psychological map of the world an integrative model of political relations. Thus the path marked out on the

Continent would be followed in Asia, North America, Central and Latin America, central Europe, and parts of Africa. "Europe," in sum, was to be "only a stage on the way to the organized world of tomorrow."[1]

Reason of State, Old and New

The decline of the nation-state in Western Europe has less to do with the Cold War than it does with the world war that preceded it, and, in effect, caused it. Neither the start of World War II in 1939 nor its end in 1945 prompted an orgy of nationalist sentiment comparable to what had occurred before and after World War I. The outbreak of war in 1914 unleashed virulent public outbursts of vibrant patriotism aimed at revanche or status. But it was the decay of nationalism that facilitated Hitler's early occupation of much of Europe in 1939, and it was left to two gigantic multinational states to liberate the Continent in 1945.[2] After the war, Winston Churchill and Charles de Gaulle, the two political giants who had salvaged the dignity of their countries during the war years, were promptly dismissed by their own peoples. Both before and after the war, the majority in either nation had little use for a vision that pretended to justify the personal horrors of the moment with memories of past national greatness. After 1945 boundaries were redrawn, populations moved, states seized, flags and anthems changed, empires abandoned and others seized, rarely causing more than a ripple in popular sentiment.

Western democracies on the European continent now shared a dirty family secret that their political leaders learned to acknowledge slowly and to accept reluctantly: that their nations could no longer suffice to fulfill their people's lives. There was more to this than the experience of military defeat. The war had been waged with enough brutality to humiliate its protagonists, despondent losers and alleged winners alike, all deeply if not evenly.

For many centuries before, the nations of Europe had not only constituted a closed political order generally safe from aggression or domination from any other nation except one of their own. They had also built a civilization of their own, one that they felt compelled to export elsewhere as the so-called burden of their rank. But now their once-proud people were brought together in an implicit community of shame for what they had done to each other, and in an explicit community of fear for what might still await them. Their postwar craving for integration is, therefore, not difficult to comprehend: it was a rebellion against the abject conditions that prevailed in 1945. Churchill's stirring call at Zurich in September 1946 that Europe arise from its unhappiness, rebuild its ruins, and regain its freedom by sharing its common values and its common inheritance in "a kind of United States of Europe" was universally hailed by Europeans. "Why," asked Churchill, "should there not be a European group which could give a sense of enlarged patriotism and common citizenship to the distracted peoples of this mighty continent?" The question was especially telling, since it was raised by a European statesman whose country was the only one in Europe where the experience of war had strengthened rather than discredited its people's allegiance to the nation-state. In France, Italy, and Germany, new constitutions made room for a delegation of national sovereignty to the kind of European group evoked by Churchill. And whatever their motives and whatever their outcomes, the initiatives for European unity that were launched in the latter part of the 1940s and during much of the following decade were truly grandiose.

Clearly, nation-states cannot be expected to relinquish lightly their sovereignty, or their values, to some faceless foreign technocrats. As reconstruction from the war began, and as memories of the killing faded, these early initiatives mostly proved to be false starts. But after the European Defense Community had been rejected, the relaunching of Europe that started with the Rome Treaty in 1957 coincided with another wave of nationalist decline that had to do with the collapse of the European empires. To be sure, when Belgium, France, and Holland signed the treaty, they still clung to imperial ambitions that had already been shattered for two of their three other partners, Germany and Italy. But the European Economic Community that came to life in subsequent years soon became an implicit compensation for the new losses suffered by its members outside of Europe. These empires had been an essential part of each European nation's image of itself. Deprived of their overseas territories, these nations were denied the body and the global stature to which they had grown accustomed. However grudgingly, they would have to learn to accommodate a new, more modest station.

History is littered with countless wars waged in order to avoid or avenge losses of national sovereignty less significant than those that have been imposed by the European Community on its members. In the face of this history, even now, after forty years, the European passage away from the nation-state offers little prospect of a shortcut. As before, as always, the journey requires a search through many tedious detours and apparent dead ends. They cannot and should not be avoided. For these provide each state with the time needed to reassure its populace and to foster the illusion that it still has a choice.

Paradoxically, the kind of opposition to the European process mounted by Prime Minister Margaret Thatcher in the 1980s—or by President Charles de Gaulle in the 1960s—exerts a constructive effect on "Europe." Even as it articulates misgivings and concerns often shared by the other member-states, this opposition helps unite the other states against the alleged culprit. Conversely, absent a single-minded opponent to the pace or the scope of European integration, debates in the Community naturally become enormously complicated: as the lineup of all (or nearly all) against one (or more than one) is fragmented, no EC state can pass on to another the responsibility for delaying the fulfillment of any one set of objectives or the start of the next. As was the case after de Gaulle's resignation in April 1969, Thatcher's resignation in November 1990 gave way to renewed Franco-German and intra-European tensions over the Community's projects for monetary and political union. No longer could these tensions be hidden behind the convenient screen provided by one leader's acerbic, hostile, and eloquent rhetoric.

Much of the debate about "Europe" turns primarily on questions of pace and timing, as well it should. For every member-state specifically, as well as for the EC generally, there is a time for everything—joining the Community or not, broadening it or not, deepening its institutions or not. In the 1950s Britain did not participate in the Common Market because it was not ready yet. Its government and its people still believed that the Commonwealth gave it size, America gave it influence, and geography gave it security. Minutes of the cabinet meetings held in 1960 confirm that Prime Minister Harold Macmillan and his colleagues still considered the terms of the Rome Treaty unacceptable even as they prepared their bid for admission in the EEC. Even then, Britain had to overcome its illusions and confront the reality of its decline. But the reluctance it showed, then and later, was not entirely new for a country already admonished by Adam Smith, nearly two centuries earlier, "to accommodate her future views and designs to the real mediocrity of her circumstances."[3] And even after admission, these illusions continued to linger. As Thatcher reportedly described the process of EC membership, "Entry . . . consist[s] of two parts. One agreeing to a whole lot of things to get in and then, once in, trying to undo all the amazing things you agree to do in the first place."[4]

The renegotiation of the Rome Treaty sought in the European Parliament's draft for European union had almost no realistic chance of adoption without French support. In 1963 the European Assembly's attempt to gain power over both the Council of Ministers and the European Commission was rejected by the French as readily as had been its proposal, in February 1961, that it be elected by direct universal suffrage. In 1965 the Commission's attempt to end the unanimity rule, and thus bypass the French veto, was promptly defeated by de Gaulle. In late 1969 Georges Pompidou's proposal for monetary union still distinguished between two objectives: to integrate the economies of the member-states with the new and even bold step he offered and to harmonize their policies through a loose and ambiguous process of political consultation. "The quarrel over supranationality is a false one," argued the French president in January 1971.[5] National governments could not be expected to subscribe to decisions with which they were in fundamental disagreement. To be valid for all, decisions would have to be agreed by all. Finally, in December 1974, Giscard's proposal for periodic meetings of the EC's heads of government and heads of state went in the direction of a Community of like-minded states whose ultimate authority and power could be neither usurped nor bypassed.

In May 1981 an apparently dogmatic François Mitterrand looked upon the European Community with much ambivalence. During the long years spent in the opposition, his party had developed an elaborate economic and social blueprint for the transformation of French society. In the euphoria of an unexpectedly large victory, this blueprint was implemented rapidly. It was based on the perceived need for a strong state that could force socialist values and objectives on a hostile environment at home and abroad.[6] Yet, strapped by a global economic recession, this grand strategy quickly petered out. By June 1982 the deterioration of the French economy had forced a program of economic rigor that seemed, in many respects, more conservative than the program developed by Prime Minister Raymond Barre during the latter years of the Giscard presidency. Thus denied the prospect of implementing a program based on the socialist ideals that had shaped his rise to national power, Mitterrand returned to a European vocation that had gained him Jean Monnet's support for the 1965 presidential elections, after his relentless criticism of de Gaulle's policy toward a Community whose emergence Mitterrand had also favored during the years of the Fourth Republic.[7]

In May 1984 France's endorsement of the European Parliament's draft treaty, including its basic premise of majority voting in the Council, placed the draft firmly on the Council's agenda, that is, where it mattered.[8] Moreover, the deliberate emphasis placed by Mitterrand on the prior resolution of the questions that divided the Community most passionately—including Britain's contribution to the EC budget, as well as Spain's and Portugal's requests for EC membership (which were all settled at last at the Fontainebleau summit in June 1984)—put additional pressure on Britain to accept an intergovernmental conference of member-states to decide on reforms that would be developed by an ad hoc preparatory committee. Faced with a Franco-German entente on perhaps the only EC issue over which Britain and France were usually in agreement, Thatcher was not ready to risk isolation from her EC partners by staying away from the conference—whether or not she fully understood that such a conference could be called by a simple majority of the EC countries.[9] It was not, therefore, Thatcher who changed Britain's traditional position on Europe, but Mitterrand who changed that of France. The French, by endorsing at last their partners' calls for institutional reform, became the catalyst for the very changes they had so fiercely opposed in the past.

One can only imagine, of course, what the Common Market might have become had Britain escaped France's opposition earlier. Nevertheless, the struggles that stalled "Europe" in the 1970s suggest how much of a drag the British government might have been. From the time Britain entered the EC until 1984, complaints over its share of the Community's budget either dominated or menaced the discussions held in fifteen EC summits. Conversely, while Britain stayed out in the 1960s, French policies did not prevent or slow down the reduction of tariffs and the termination of trade quotas among the Six scheduled by the Rome Treaty.

In the 1960s, as now in the 1990s, the European institutions had to be strengthened before their membership could be enlarged. In the 1970s, as later in the 1980s, lingering issues of enlargement had to be resolved before the next attempt at strengthening the institutions could be launched. In other words, the Community becomes wider (meaning more, and generally less powerful, members) as a prerequisite to becoming deeper (meaning more, and more powerful, institutions). Agreement to do the former, after many years of negotiations, is a political compromise achieved in order to launch the latter, after many years of opposition. Once the deal has been consummated, however, there is little room for additional expansion until the institutions have been strengthened. Thus, building the Common Market in the 1960s left no room for new members, including Britain. But seeking an economic and monetary union required a French willingness to agree to new members, including Denmark and Ireland, as part of the compromise that enabled President Pompidou to gain Chancellor Brandt's support in 1969. The same was true in the 1980s, when widening the Community from ten to twelve members—which had not been anticipated when France had favored

Greece's admission during the discussions over the organization of the EMS—was a prerequisite to agreement over the Single European Act. By a same logic, a monetary union and progress on political union in the 1990s required first a final resolution of the EC's negotiations with the EFTA countries, in October 1991, as a first step toward full membership later in the decade.

As they fight a process that they can no longer do without, the nations of Western Europe respond to challenges of efficiency and relevance. They know that they have become too small, and, despite their remarkable recovery from the devastating wars fought in this century, that they have remained too weak to compete effectively with, or stand effectively against, their rivals and adversaries abroad. They are sapped, therefore, by the evidence of their own failure— failure, that is, to continue to go it alone, to remain sufficiently competitive, economically and militarily, to provide their populace with the well-being and the security to which they aspire. But by going it together with the Community, EC nations are also sapped increasingly by the evidence of their success—success, that is, in promoting a habit of cooperation that transcends citizens' allegiance to their own historical group.

Every bit of bad news about Europe is not bad for "Europe," since it can provide EC members with further incentives for renewing their momentum toward additional integration. Conversely, neither is all good news good, since it invites EC members to complacency. In this context the logic of "Europe" defies logic itself: the architects' blueprints have little to do with grand theories of economic and political integration. Standards set by theory alone might well have voided the Common Market of the Six before it was organized. By the theoretical standards set up for so-called optimal-currency areas, it might well be argued, as it was by many, that the European Monetary System should not have been launched, let alone been successful, and steps toward economic and monetary union should not now be envisioned, let alone implemented.

Nor is "Europe" the result of a collective and sustained determi- nation to invent a future that is not yet imminent. No specific vision of the future drives today's actions—none, that is, that can be encapsulated in a neat formula, where words have a precise and certain meaning for all. As Jean Monnet aptly concluded late in his life, "The true political authority which the democracies of Europe will one day establish still has to be conceived and built."[10] Nor can any future, however broadly outlined, be locked into a timetable that would be construed as a binding and irreversible commitment—none, that is, that cannot accommodate delays. Nor, finally, can any timetable, however loose, be made the arbiter of the effectiveness with which the initial objectives are achieved. Conditioning these objectives is a collective will to do, which responds to the aspirations of an unknown future. Slowing their implementation is a general will to enforce, which obeys the known necessities of the present. To narrate and reconstruct the processes by which both interact is to rediscover the elements of national experience, need, tradition, and interest that caused failure at a given time without compromising success later on.

Driving the process of integration in Western Europe after each failure is a political logic of community-building that makes German urban dwellers subsidize French farmers and that leads both to contribute to the regional development of Greece, Ireland, southern Italy, or Portugal. Most broadly, this political logic finds the cumulative gains of the process over time superior to its costs at any one time: economic gains that enhance growth and prosperity for all of its members; political gains that strengthen further their democratic foundation and stability; and security gains that also provide plausible grounds for the revival of their status in the world. In turn, the accumulation of these gains has been conducive to a revised social contract in which the citizen's allegiance, once owed almost exclusively to the nation-state, is now often extended to the Community as well.

Revising the Social Contract

The economic benefits brought by the European Common Market to its members have been significant. According to some calculations, the output of EC countries was 2.3 percent higher in 1972, and 5.9 percent higher in 1981, than it would have been without the Common Market, before and after the enlargement in 1973, respectively.[11] Specific numbers can be questioned, of course. But whatever they are, few still question the assumption that the Common Market has been generally good to its members. Most broadly, it helped translate the economic recovery of the 1950s into the relative affluence of the 1960s; it helped preserve much of this affluence during the years of economic stagnation in the 1970s; and it is now serving as the framework of Europe's attempt to regain a competitiveness lost to the United States and other industrial countries in Asia.

To be sure, at any one time some member-states have gained more from the Community than others. There have been winners and there have been losers: from country to country, and, within each country, from region to region and from sector to sector. Perfect economic convergence is beyond reach. It could not be achieved in the past and will not be achieved in the future. Yet a single economic market can accommodate different rates of growth and different levels of development for its members over prolonged periods of time. In the United States, states and regions that are relative losers in a phase of economic upswing often emerge as relative winners in the economic downturn that follows, depending on circumstances over which they exert limited control: high or low energy prices, fluctuations in defense expenditures, or even the effectiveness of political leadership at the local level, for example. In the Community, too, Holland and Belgium, as well as Italy, probably gained more from the EEC during its first decade than they did the following decade, after the EEC had grown from six to nine members. All three countries were better prepared than France and Germany to absorb the significant trade expansion caused by the Common Market and the GATT rounds of tariff reduction. The reverse is probably true for the post-1973 period, however. By then, an offsetting increase in the propensity to import reduced these early advantages, especially for the Benelux countries, and France emerged as the country that gained the most from the Common Market relative to its partners.[12]

The same tendency toward balance can be observed in other facets of the Community's economic life. Japan, having learned the intricacies of doing business with the West in the United States, chose Britain as its favorite partner in Europe. That nation still receives the largest share of Japan's direct investment in the European Community: nearly $2.5 billion in 1987, more than the total of Japanese direct investments for the whole of the Community minus Luxemburg (about $2.3 billion). In 1990 Japan's direct investment in Britain grew to $6.8 billion and nearly matched its direct investment in Asia.[13]

However, Britain's privileged relationship with Japan is losing its nearly exclusive character. Already, a more open and less confrontational Community is enabling Japanese firms to aspire to a wider distribution of their holdings throughout the single market, which Japanese business is discovering in the 1990s as eagerly as U.S. business discovered the Common Market in the 1960s. Meanwhile, foreign investments in Britain by EC firms remain lower than, say, in Spain and in France, as the expansion of the Community to the South and new conditions in the East improve these countries' competitive position relative to Britain.

The point is that intra-Community conflicts reflecting fears of both the national and sectoral impact of the 1992 program, as well as local and societal apprehensions over its human consequences, are intrinsic features of community-building. In the EC these are neither unique nor new. General gains forecast for the twelve member-states cannot exclude severe losses in some of these states relative to others, and, within most states, in some specific regions relative to others. Understandably, every EC country wants to concede less to, and hopes to gain more from, the Community: a larger share of international investments, better access to the EC development funds, strengthened protection from competition. Such aspirations on the part of every EC country are woven into the many priorities and uneven dependencies that shape its domestic policies: not only employment but also inflation, commodity prices, and monetary stability, as well as the militancy of labor unions, the appeal of extremist ideologies, oil and trade dependencies, and so forth.

From conflict to conflict, compromises struck within the Community are compromises that are also struck at home, on the assumption that their more painful consequences will not last and that their benefits will be progressively balanced. After each compromise, the process is often derailed if, and when, the price of compromise proves to be, or becomes, politically unsustainable. A reminder of how quickly pressures can build was shown in 1991, when an economic downturn prompted renewed calls for aid from the state, and protection from the Commission, for such key sectors as electronics, cars, aerospace, and air transportation. As the Commission is motivated by the will to build "Europe" more than by any conviction about the merits of free trade and the like, these calls are unlikely to be ignored for too long, thereby introducing new conflicts until the next compromise is struck.

"What is Europe now?" asked Winston Churchill in mid-1947. Churchill's answer—"It is a rubble heap, a charnel house, a breeding ground of pestilence and hate"—provides much-needed perspective on the extraordinary progress achieved since that time by each of the countries of Western Europe separately and, within the context of the Community, collectively. These achievements are about much more than economic recovery. They are also about the democratic institutions and practices that have characterized the development of Western Europe since the end of World War II.

The postwar political settlements were expected to be protracted and difficult to achieve. They would involve far more than "the twelve dozen traitors, twelve hundred cowards, and twelve thousand idiots" whom de Gaulle judged responsible for France's wartime debacle.[14] In 1957 a majority of the six charter members of the EEC still suffered from significant domestic instabilities. An interlude of political calm came later, with France's Fifth Republic in 1958 (and a new constitution in 1962), the transformation of West Germany's Social Democratic Party in 1959 (and the first coalition government in 1967), and the opening to the Left in Italy in the early 1960s (and the transformation of the Italian Communist Party). After that, the EC set a standard of democratic stability that was made a prerequisite for membership and that delayed the admission of Greece, Portugal, and Spain until the 1980s.

As the Cold War came to an end, the countries of Western Europe showed an unprecedented ability to absorb new political shocks without much turmoil. In 1979-85 Britain turned to the Right with Margaret Thatcher, France turned to the Left with François Mitterrand, the Federal Republic turned to the Right with Helmut Kohl, and Italy turned away from the christian democrats with Bettino Craxi, without causing the sort of political eruptions that were experienced in 1947. Indeed, not only in these countries but also in all other EC countries, the deep ideological divisions that defined the grand political battles of the past have been sunk into a political melting pot that leaves little space for extremisms. Largely gone is the dogmatic content of the socialist parties in France, Italy, or Spain, for example. Mostly gone are the communist parties, which in the mid-1970s were still feared as a potent force in Western Europe. Governments now travel light, without the ideological baggage of the past. Elections used to be waged on issues that involved no less than the survival of the regime. They are now waged on more pragmatic questions of management and competence, as the outgoing government is subjected to a closer scrutiny of its performance in office. In this context the Community has strengthened the nation-state not only because of the political stability that accompanied the economic gains it brought, but also because responsibility for some of the difficult tasks once performed by the state can now be passed on to the Community, or neglected in its name.

Thus the imperatives of "Europe" and the dictates of European unity have become a perfect alibi for EC governments, which can take actions that are otherwise opposed most adamantly by their electoral clienteles. Europe-92 helps a socialist government in France justify the reform of a tax system seen by French business as one of the most illogical and least profitable in the world. Behind the political cover of Europe-92, Belgium manages a decentralization of power that has helped solve old linguistic quibbles between the Flemish and Francophones. In Spain the Community justifies the rethinking of an agricultural sector that still ranks among the least efficient in Europe. In Portugal EC membership has had more impact than the revolution that ended three decades of dictatorship. From

Sweden to Austria, even nonmembers now display the Community flag, as they choose to adjust to its rules long before the fact of membership makes this a necessity.

If the actions of the nation-state in Europe have been increasingly influenced by the European Community, the actions of the latter have also become increasingly inspired by private businesses in each country of Europe. At the beginning of the 1980s Europe's diminishing share of global trade was viewed as a symptom of the reduced international competitiveness of its export industries, especially in the vital high-technology sector, including those in the Federal Republic (though admittedly to a smaller degree).[15] In this context the prospects of a single market brought European industrialists into the political marketplace of Europe as no other initiative about or from the European Community had done over the previous four decades. "European companies should not expect politicians alone to promote further integration in Europe," claimed Carlo de Benedetti, Olivetti's chief executive officer in 1984. The approach he advocated, with other leading industrialists, was "change or die."[16] A political vision limited to the boundaries of the state would deny European corporations the global dimension without which even their national dimension could not be maintained, with or without the help of the European Commission.

"Support for integration is no longer confined to dreamers and old-fashioned romantics," later claimed the Commission. "It is coming from pragmatic Europeans, confronted day in day out with the absurdity of 12 national markets every bit as compartmentalized as they were in medieval times."[17] Buoyed by a U.S.-driven economic expansion, encouraged by the stability brought by the German-led EMS, and strengthened by high earnings (predictably a good indicator of corporate confidence), European industrialists strengthened the Commission's (and their governments') interest in ending market fragmentation. In anticipation of a single market that would permit the economies associated with large-scale production, they themselves engaged in various modes of corporate restructuring designed to facilitate the rise of pan-European conglomerates able to compete effectively with their American and Asian rivals in the European and world markets. As argued by de Benedetti, the organization of the single market was made possible "not by politicians, but by businesses determined to revive Europe as an industrial power and to open up to international markets."[18] The leap forward of 1992 was planned in the European Parliament, but it was primarily engineered by these "pragmatists" from the private sector. Coached by the Delors-led technocrats in Brussels they were now ready to compete in the new European stadium envisioned by the romantics *à la* Monnet of the postwar years.

Making Europe Competitive

In the early 1960s, notwithstanding America's competitive dominance at the time, the organization of a common economic market in one of the world's largest trade areas created apprehension across the Atlantic. Many in the United States feared the effect that a united Europe would have on the demand for U.S. exports, not only in Europe but worldwide, as well as the impact of a united Europe on foreign exports, which the closed EEC markets might divert toward the United States. These fears—exaggerated but not all unwarranted—introduced sharp transatlantic commercial rivalries and political conflicts that have not eased as the Community has grown and matured.

With the single market, too, concerns over a European fortress that might challenge the U.S. faith in a liberal world economy have been pronounced. The decline of the American economy, relative to the overwhelming dominance it enjoyed after World War II, leaves the United States more vulnerable to Europe's ambition to regain its competitiveness at a time when U.S. industry already finds it difficult to face its competitors from Japan and other newly industrialized countries in Asia. Moreover, the erosion of the Soviet military threat reduces the relevance of an American strategy that leveraged the U.S. contribution to European security to manage economic ties with Europe—thus linking burden-sharing in security relations and profit-sharing in economic relations.[19]

As the European Commission proceeds with the organization of a single market, calls from national capitals for an orderly transition raise the specter of regulations specifying superficial levels of market penetration by non-EC exporters. Addressed to different business sectors depending on their point of origin, these calls claim free trade legitimacy with vague references to the need for comparable competitive opportunities. They suggest that even in, and especially because of, an open market, "national champions"—that is, corporate leaders who dominate one major sector in an EC country—will remain shielded with all kinds of subsidies aimed at defeating, or at least containing, the competition of foreign subsidiaries or foreign exporters.

These instincts for market protection are real, of course. They have been an intrinsic component of the Community's history and an important feature of the economic history of most of the nation-states that compose the EC. In the 1970s, after the Tokyo Round of tariff reductions, access to the EC's market for countries without the same leverage as the United States ceased to be shaped by general rules of trade. Instead, it became determined mostly by a series of administrative and negotiated decisions that singled out countries and products for special treatment and opened the door to nontariff trade interventions of all kinds: in 1987 a World Bank study counted eleven separate categories of EC preferences for selected Third World countries.[20] No doubt, many new categories will be developed in coming years for the newly liberated countries of central and Eastern Europe and newly independent Soviet republics.

Yet perceptions of a "Fortress Europe" are exaggerated. They have become as shallow as the perceptions of an emerging "Fortress America" that originate in Europe. Just as the United States is too entangled in the world to turn away from it politically, Europe is far too much involved with the rest of the world to turn away from it economically. Debates in the Community and each member-state can only be about periods of transition that will inevitably end.

The future of "Europe" spells more trade openness not less, fewer government subsidies not more, and more competition not less. The single market does not build the outer walls of a fortress but frames instead the lattice of a large commercial sieve. There were early fears that the single market would rely on product standards, testing, and certification to control the entry of U.S. (and other non-EC) products, whether inadvertently or by design. Such procedures, U.S. exporters warned, would limit their ability to perform competitively in the single market. These fears, however, have proved mostly unfounded. In 1989 U.S. exporters and their technical experts were allowed ad hoc access to the main European standards committees. And the Commission agreed to negotiate with the United States mutual recognition of testing and certification procedures. Hence the satisfaction expressed by U.S. Secretary of Commerce Robert Mosbacher, just twelve months after he had asked bitterly for an observer seat at the Community: "The Commerce Department and the EC," he declared in early 1990, "have reached agreements on standards, testing and certification issues which have advanced the interests of American companies."[21]

In this area, as in many others, tensions between the EC and the United States will ultimately depend less on the European Commission than on how convincingly the European Council and the Council of Ministers adopt the Commission's directives, how quickly the member-states turned these into national legislation, and how effectively the Court of Justice enforces them. Away from the Commission, protection remains tempting and national capitals can obstruct individually whatever has been agreed collectively in Brussels. Thus, EC directives for 1992 must be debated in and by each parliamentary body, where emerge new ambiguities that provide for more conflicts and cause further delays. As ratification of each directive is needed from all twelve EC countries before it becomes Community law, these debates add to the uncertainties faced by foreign exporters in preparing for the single market. For a time at least, local producers find in these delays the protection they still need while they improve the competitiveness they sorely lack.

For all the attention they received, the heavy subsidies provided by the Commission and the member states through various collaborative research and development (R&D) programs in the sectors of information technology and communications have had limited impact and few tangible results.[22] Designed to facilitate pre-competitive research and encourage corporate partnerships in product-oriented R&D on a Europe-wide scale, these programs were expected to be less costly and more effective than the alternative, which required national subsidies for overlapping R&D among and within EC countries.[23] With the programs envisioned on behalf of a European technological community producing few new and lasting joint ventures, and few new and competitive products, European companies in leading growth sectors of high technology have remained intrinsically weak.[24] At best, these programs helped remove temporarily the barriers that separate national champions in Europe, and they stimulated flows of technical information among them—at least until expiration of the collaborative project to which they were committed. But the protection extended by these subsidies has not been translated into larger and more profitable world market shares, and the Commission's preference now leans toward reducing these subsidies, whatever their source, rather than increasing or even sustaining them.

Whatever remains of the competitive ranking of leading EC electronics firms owes a great deal to local and European sales painfully nurtured by the preferential treatment they receive from their governments and the European Commission. After 1992 this treatment will eventually diminish, and Europe's presence in the computer industry is likely to become contingent upon developing innovative niches built on specialty products.[25] Already, Europe's $35 billion trade deficit in electronics is expected to grow, and possibly double, during the eight to ten years it might take for suppliers from the United States and Asia to assert their control in the post-1992 single market.

As they struggle to stay alive, most of the largest European computer companies face a serious financial and managerial crisis that raises legitimate doubts about their ability to maintain independent capacity. Restructuring programs, including sharp cutbacks in jobs, have remained generally insufficient to improve competitiveness outside of whatever remains of the firm's protected market. Based on sales per employees in mid-1990 (figures that, admittedly, are not entirely comparable), Siemens, the largest European firm in electronics after its takeover of Nixdorf, employed about the same work force as IBM but generated only half of IBM's total sales.[26] That in recent years Europe would have bred few new computer companies—except in software and services—is also a good illustration of the technological edge maintained by non-EC firms over their EC rivals: starting with less than $20 million in European sales in 1984, America's Compaq became Europe's second supplier of business personal computers in five years, behind only IBM and ahead of Italy's Olivetti.

Launched as another compensating scheme for each participant's own weaknesses, alliances between the EC's national champions have been defensive alliances of convenience aimed at the preservation of dwindling market shares in Europe. In late 1990, for example, the alliance between Italy's Fiat and France's Compagnie Générale d'Electricité (CGE) gave Alcatel, CGE's main source of business, control of Telettra, Fiat's telecommunications subsidiary. Since Telettra was strongest in Italy and Spain, where Alcatel was weakest, the logic of this asset swap between the two European giants was transparent. The deal also linked the high-speed trains built by Fiat's Ferroviara and CGE's Alsthom, thereby strengthening Fiat's position for the supply of rolling stock for the Channel tunnel—a much-needed gain, given Fiat's notable weakness in Britain, where Japan's Fujitsu, firmly implanted in Britain after its acquisition of ICL, also hoped to distribute its own transmissions equipment.[27]

These alliances do not alleviate a legacy of mutual suspicion and rivalry among the new partners in the European Community. In the mid-1980s, for example, the so-called "Mega project" linked Germany's Siemens and Holland's Philips for the development of a more powerful and less expensive memory chip.[28] The price paid for regaining a modest measure of competitiveness on the Continent proved considerable, however. Although the Franco-Italian team of SGS-Thomson joined these R&D efforts, the three main European chip makers lacked the scale needed to achieve competitiveness and profitability in their semiconductor activities: any one of the three biggest Japanese producers had a turnover equal to their combined output. Yet, with losses mounting accordingly, Philips, SGS-Thomson, and Siemens remained unable to overcome their hostility and merge their operations. In September 1990, therefore, Philips, a corporate leader in seeking and receiving aid and protection, retreated from past lofty goals and reduced significantly its involvement in semiconductor research and production at a time when its worldwide sales of semiconductors were actually rising. As Siemens and SGS-Thomson also contemplate significant losses, similar rollbacks by either or both would leave Europe without an indigenous semiconductor producer of adequate size.

Finally, such alliances do not reconcile the different corporate philosophies embraced by each partner. Britain's traditional financial culture expects and even requires short-term profitability, but Germany's reputation for engineering excellence emphasizes long-term research. Both clashed after the controversial takeover by General Electric and Siemens of Plessey, a British electronics concern, in late 1988.[29] These cultural gaps exist even when the corporate alliance groups two firms from the same country. Thus Siemens's acquisition of Nixdorf was partly motivated by the latter's market presence in Britain, France, and Spain, all markets where Siemens's relative weakness needed quick reinforcement. But the two companies found it difficult to reconcile their differences in approach to customer support, in part conditioned by Siemens's emphasis on small-scale systems.

In short, neither state subsidies nor joint programs from the European Community, nor, finally, a growing number of mergers, joint ventures, equity swaps, and other corporate arrangements, have been conducive to the emergence of new pan-European giants. Instead, the repeated failures of intra-European arrangements have exposed a European preference for regaining lost competitiveness through agreements with non-EC firms. Relative to other competitors, teaming up with a powerful American or Japanese partner gives the national champion much-needed capital, new technologies, or instant access to the global marketplace.[30] In 1990 the takeover of Britain's ICL by Japan's Fujitsu, for example, came after earlier attempts to weld ICL with Olivetti and Nixdorf had failed, primarily over issues of management control. It was especially significant, since ICL had emerged as a corporate leader in systems integration, a leading area of corporate profitability for computer makers in the 1990s. In the same context Siemens chose the American route (IBM) after it had briefly considered Japan's Toshiba and dismissed Thomson's advances.

The point common to these examples is that over time the 1992 process is likely to diminish further the ability, and even the will, of European states to protect their national markets, not only against other EC countries but also against non-EC countries outside of Europe. This trend is manifesting itself even in the defense sector, which is affected only indirectly by the 1992 program. As defense markets are reduced everywhere, earlier national priorities become increasingly fuzzy, and national champions that are threatened with extinction look for new partners, in or out of Europe, even as they gobble up smaller national producers. Thus, Eurocopter grows out of the merger of helicopter activities between France's Aerospatiale and Deutsche Aerospace; Eurodynamics is tied to the continued effort by Thomson and British Aerospace to link their activities in the development of tactical missiles. This new corporate context, which is shaped by commercial rather than political considerations, also reduces the state's ability to pursue an independent defense policy, and it may act as a catalyst for a future European defense policy.

In sum, during and beyond the organization of a single market among the twelve EC countries, "Europe" will not construct a fortress, which, by definition, would have to be viewed as impregnable. Instead, as the process unfolds, "Europe" is becoming a platform that national champions use to emerge as global competitors if they can or to corral local partners if they must.[31] A European platform need not be occupied only by Europeans, however. That IBM would have been allowed by the Commission to collaborate with some of its most significant R&D projects shows that EC countries understand that in many areas Europe's last best hope may lie anywhere but in Brussels. That ICL, after it was acquired by Fujitsu, would have been removed from the European Information Technology

Round Table, a lobby group that it helped form a decade earlier, confirms the limits of EC tolerance and, possibly, the direction of its preferences. Everything else being equal, it would rather team up with the United States than with Japan. Yet 1991 negotiations between France's Bull Groupe and Japan's NEC, resumed with the approval of French Prime Minister Edith Cresson, also show that in business, as in other matters, preferences alone do not suffice. Beyond Europe-92, the rules of a competitive *ménage à trois* among American, Japanese, and EC firms have not been devised and its results cannot yet be predicted.

Whole and Free?

Paradoxically, the "whole and free" Europe that President Bush welcomed after the Cold War is more real at the macropolitical level, where it is institutionally least developed, than at the microeconomic level, where it has become institutionally most refined. Or, to put it differently, thirty-five years after the Rome Treaty, historical tensions and national rivalries in Western Europe—say, between France and Germany—have faded more convincingly than tensions between dominant companies in these countries—say, between France's Thomson and Germany's Siemens. And while the revolutions of 1989 in Eastern Europe and of 1991 in the Soviet Union have moved the Continent closer to democratic freedom than ever before, these revolutions have also exposed wide divisions between the affluence and the stability that prevail in the West and the poverty and uncertainties that exist in the East.

For at least one half of Europe, the Cold War proved to be constructive. Although it ended too soon to settle divisions between nationalities and ethnic groups in Eastern Europe, it lasted long enough to resolve historical conflicts between the nation-states of Western Europe. How could a war between any two members of the European Community now be imagined? By a similar logic, a few years of shared EC membership would do more to reduce tensions between Greece and Turkey than nearly four decades of common membership in NATO, and it is at least arguable that an early offer of closer ties with the Community might have avoided civil war in Yugoslavia in 1991.

Moreover, a Community that has liberated its members from the hostilities that brought them to war every so often has also blurred the hierarchy that used to divide them. How else could the smaller countries in Western Europe be heard? Over issues that still require unanimity, their voice is no less significant than that of their larger, bigger, and stronger partners in the Community. Their presidencies of the European Council are assumed with no less regularity than for other states, and, depending on the calendar of European integration, with no less significance. To be sure, over some of the more significant issues the bigger EC countries can still pull rank from within the Community or in representing it in the world without. Arguably, the EC might have mediated the civil war in Yugoslavia more effectively had it been led by the three largest EC members rather than three of the smallest. Paradoxically, the pooling of sovereignty enhances the sovereignty of the weak by making it the equal of the strong, for those moments at least when the voice it carries is that of the Community. Membership has its privileges, as perceptions of rank and status lose some, or much, of their past significance.

In Eastern Europe conflicts and inequalities, within and between states, were neglected but not solved. There, it is almost as if the past forty years never happened. Neither the fears that grew out of the communist revolutions of 1945-48 nor the hopes associated with the anticommunist revolutions of 1989-90 have proved to be long lasting. Everywhere, history revives deeper forces that delve even further into the past than the living memories of the Cold War: back to the authoritarian temptations of the interwar years (a period that barely amounted to half of the Cold War era); back to the instabilities that followed peacemaking at Versailles in 1919; back to the territorial ambitions that shaped the descent to war in 1914; back to the consequences of Germany's unification in 1871; back to the democratic upheavals and failures of 1848; and back to the aspirations for a restored European order after the Napoleonic wars in 1815.

That the Cold War would have been won to resurrect history rather than to end it is hardly a cause for joy. Age-old memories of central and Eastern Europe are rarely happy. A region that is still traumatized by the collapse of Austria-Hungary and the Ottoman Empire must now face the territorial consequences of the dismemberment of the Soviet empire. Changes in Eastern Europe have resurrected conflicts that were hidden behind the unifying impact of ideology. Changes in the Soviet Union threaten to unleash any number of independent republics that were buried under the weight of Russia for many years before they were forced into the Soviet Union. The Europe that is emerging from the Cold War may well be a Europe that is free. But it is not one that is whole. Nor is it likely to remain at peace.

The gap between the economically affluent and politically stable community of the Twelve in Western Europe and the economically despondent and politically fragile countries of the former communist states in Eastern Europe is huge. As the last remnants of the old order are shoved aside, this gap cannot be dismissed as the logical fate of inept and misguided policies. Worse yet, however the East-West gap might be measured, it is already wide and large and is growing even wider and larger, exposing a continental fault line that threatens to erupt into a political earthquake of some consequence. For the European Community, the 1992 single market will bring more wealth and more economic and political homogeneity to countries that are already wealthy and homogeneous: a 2.5 to 6.5 percent gain in output, according to EC estimates that may well prove to be conservative.[32] For their brethren in the East, the conversion to democracy and free market economies will continue to cause more poverty and more divisions in countries that are already poor and divided.

Now and for many years to come, the Third World begins in Eastern Europe: their people threaten the European Community with millions of refugees in countries where the reaction to immigrants from North Africa confirm that they no longer want any. In what used to be the Soviet Union, 60 million people live in republics other than their own. Elsewhere—in Albania, Bulgaria, and

Romania—ethnic minorities are, or may become, less and less welcome. In Yugoslavia, force has been used to make the point. Everywhere, millions of people are losing jobs for which the old regime had pledged a lifetime guarantee: some estimates envision as many as 15 million unemployed in central and Eastern Europe, and 30 to 40 million in the Soviet Union, by 1994. Under circumstances of growing anarchy, strife, and poverty, inducing these people to stay home will be an easy task neither for their governments nor for those of Western Europe.

Whether Mikhail Gorbachev ever knew what he was doing with and to the Soviet empire he inherited is doubtful. Most probably, he displayed considerable skill in responding to the consequences, never foreseen, of each wave of reform he started after rising to power in 1985. At first his adjustments were quick and even reasonable. As he made them, Gorbachev enhanced his stature in the West, where the Soviet leader was praised as a radical. Soon, however, a perverse logic undermined the relative success of Gorbachev's opening to the West: the more the Soviet leader conceded in Eastern Europe and elsewhere, the weaker his hold became on whatever was left of the Soviet empire, and, accordingly, his leverage in the West diminished. In turn, the miscalculations that produced each new adjustment predictably diminished his own popularity at home, where the Soviet leader was criticized as a moderate. The more the Soviet people were led by Gorbachev himself into rebelling against their past, the less they understood the future he intended to build, and the more they turned to the alternative allegedly offered by the republics.

Around the world, the Soviet Union now controls too little space to lead the life of a superpower. What else could the Soviet Union concede, now that its leadership has abandoned its empire, and where else could it regain the military credibility needed to reconstruct it? Around the country, there is too much to be done before a new democratic system emerges in whatever remains of the Soviet Union: where else could the central leadership gain the political credibility needed to construct it? In short, by the time of the aborted coup of August 1991, Gorbachev had outlived his usefulness, both because of how much he did abroad and how little he did at home.

At best, the coup restored some of that usefulness: moderating the pace of disintegration at home by providing disparate republics with the remnants of a central authority, and containing the consequences of disorder abroad by giving other countries, especially the United States, a single interlocutor over issues of arms control. But even such a modest restoration of Gorbachev's relevance cannot be expected to last much longer, notwithstanding the unavailability of options in the USSR and within each of its republics.

History will not dismiss Gorbachev's personal contribution. As de Gaulle would have put it, the Soviet leader was "a man of consequence." In Eastern Europe, especially, he staged the dramas of 1989 almost single-handedly. Not only did Gorbachev choose to acquiesce to change instead of using force to smash it when action was still possible, he also condoned change as the belated evidence of his own commitment to reform at home. Yet, whatever Gorbachev may have had in mind, the revolutions undertaken by Eastern Europeans were mostly about terminating, not just reforming, their regimes and the instruments that had ruled them for the previous forty years. By the time the people took to the streets of their national capitals in search of the affluence that their governments were unable to provide, the economic stagnation that had afflicted the entire region throughout the 1980s (following the relatively good performance of the previous decade) was turning into an outright recession. Accordingly, the political rockets that gave these revolutions speed and direction soon outdistanced the Gorbachevian launcher—which was expected to propel them toward reform—and entered a trajectory defined by a growing public dissatisfaction with the day-to-day experience of poverty and oppression.

The anguish and sheer exasperation of the populace left their rulers with little choice. Either they would let go of their people, or the people would let go of their regimes. Liberation from the party's oppression and its leaders' ineptitude had little to do with the rekindling of deep nationalist instincts. In Germany, especially, where nationalism would have been most feared by its neighbors, the people who vented their anger in the streets of the Democratic Republic wanted to be rich and free, like their stepbrothers in the

West. They sought to open the gate to instant prosperity through Hungary. As the growing inflow of East German immigrants appeared to threaten the delicate socioeconomic fabric in the Federal Republic, and even endangered Helmut Kohl's fragile political majority in the Federal Republic, unification became the panacea. The possibility that *Deutschland* might become *über alles* again came almost as an afterthought. Throughout, the German chancellor acted primarily out of economic necessity and political expediency. His ill-considered offer of a one-for-one currency swap had more to do with the welfare of his party than of either part of his country.

As events came to show, Kohl's decision to move ahead with Germany's unification, whatever its economic cost, was even more politically right than he knew or suspected at the time. Had he spurned the opportunity that presented itself so very unexpectedly in late 1989, he might have lost it altogether twelve months later, when Gorbachev showed a new sensitivity to political pressures from the Red Army and the communist party. But the economists who opposed Kohl's initiative, whatever its political benefits, also were more right than they knew or suspected at the time. They, too, probably failed to anticipate the true cost of unification, particularly since there was no time to achieve a semblance of economic convergence before the implementation of economic and monetary union for the entire country.

Not just in East Germany but throughout the region, events moved at an extraordinary pace, as new developments anywhere had a clear and immediate impact everywhere else. Late in 1989 all six non-Soviet member countries of the Warsaw Pact were liberated in weeks and, with the exception of Romania, without violence. Yet all these revolutions should not be merged into one. They were different from country to country, and so were their outcomes. In Bulgaria and Romania (as well as Albania) old-fashioned dictators, never challenged before, were painfully removed. But remnants of the old regime have survived. In Czechoslovakia, Hungary, and Poland targets of these revolutions were would-be rescuers of the communist system who had failed in their efforts. The old regime has been swept away.

This is the Europe of 1919, not that of 1945. Memories of the quick collapse of the fragile parliamentary democracies that were established hastily after World War I, and the tragic consequences of this collapse two decades later, serve as a reminder of the dramas that have been staged in the West because of instabilities that began in the East. During the interwar years, the collapse of democracy in Eastern Europe resulted from the conflicts between the interests of the ruling parties and their leaders and those of the majority of the population. Significantly, these conflicts were spreading before the worldwide economic difficulties of the 1930s began to exacerbate them. Marshall Pilsudski, a self-made hero born out of the military battles of World War I, carried out his coup d'état in Poland in 1926. Evoking Poland's greatness, Pilsudski thought first of his own; calling for Poland's unity, he displayed his own intolerance for political dissent. At first, Pilsudski left some freedom to parliament. But as the economic crisis settled in, he tightened his pressure on the political parties until 1935, when the introduction of a new constitution ended the democratic charade of the previous nine years.[33]

In late 1990, too, it did not take long for Lech Walesa, another self-made hero, born of the political battles of liberation waged by the Solidarity union against Soviet oppression, to unveil the explosive potential of social and political discontent. Born out of the democratic euphoria that forced the communist party to surrender control of parliament after the elections of June 1989, the reform program launched by Prime Minister Tadeusz Mazowiecki was a brave and largely successful attempt to address an economic legacy that may have been the worst in central Europe. Widely praised abroad, Mazowiecki's program was rejected by the large majority of Poles who preferred instead the populist rhetoric used by Walesa to exploit the democratic backwardness that breeds intolerance and authoritarianism. Thus, Walesa's warning that his defeat might cause "something like civil war" had nothing to do with the democratic legitimacy of the presidential election, which the union hero of the 1980s never questioned.[34] It had to do with democracy's most fundamental principle—the opposition's right to win—and Walesa's decision to assume the exclusive right to serve as the final arbiter between society and its elected representatives.

It would be foolish to believe that, not only in Poland but elsewhere in the newly liberated states of central and Eastern Europe, four decades of political ineptitude, economic self-destruction, and national subservience could be overcome as quickly as they were during the moment of revolutionary unity in 1989. The magnitude of the recovery that is needed is not enough to measure the reality of the task ahead. Life without Moscow and without the communist party is going to challenge the tolerance of the people and their leaders. In the end, building a coherent "we" aimed at putting down the oppressor is an easier task than sustaining this collective identity against the embedded features of the nation's traditionally fragmented political loyalties. Paper constitutions and prolonged deprivation can sustain a revolution, but they do not suffice to build democratic traditions. Looming ahead of any revolutionary break with a totalitarian past is an authoritarian temptation that begins by settling accounts with the fallen bureaucracy but ends up compiling accounts with an allegedly confused society.

In short, what is perversely rediscovered is that, before falling into the Soviet empire, the countries of central and Eastern Europe were not a fulcrum of political stability and widespread prosperity. Social, religious, and ethnic intolerance and cross-border conflicts prevailed in each of these countries long before new standards of brutality and repression were set by Hitler's Germany first and Stalin's Russia next. With both now gone, the new reality is that of a region where the Cold War muted but did not end a long history of recurring conflicts: a region where states with lingering ambitions are challenged by the many nationalities they attempted to absorb within uncertain boundaries enforced during centuries of declining Ottoman rule and several decades of corrupt communist rule.

The legacy is truly terrifying. After World War II, Eastern Europe was the focus of a revolution that was imposed from Moscow and sought from above. It took forty years to undo it with a string of revolutions that were sought against Moscow's rule and driven from below. The process has just begun, however, and it will take many more years before it is completed. The goal of this process is known and widely shared, within and without the region: to create viable and modern European states worthy of admission to the European Community. How this objective is fulfilled—how peacefully, if not how quickly—may prove crucial to the stability of the European continent as a whole.

Creating such states as the required condition of a Europe that can become whole even as it is kept free cannot begin with their dismemberment, however. Although each country in the region shows distinctive political, economic, cultural, and historical features, each evolves at a pace that is affected by its neighbors, as was shown in 1919, 1945, and 1989. In this region changes begin somewhere in the name of self-determination, spread elsewhere as a disease would, and end up everywhere in ever more brutal disorders that lead nowhere. The list of past rivalries that can flare into bloody conflicts covers the entire area. The civil war in Yugoslavia is a model more than an exception: almost by definition, no state can attend to its disintegration with the decorum of democratic order.

Later, perhaps, the boundaries within which nationalities are kept together might become as insignificant as national boundaries in the European Community. But this time has not come yet. For many years, EC membership will remain a distant objective more than an immediate option for the countries that have escaped Soviet domination. Pretending otherwise is misleading. The EC has no room for broadening its membership to the East so long as it has not explored more deeply its potential for institutional development.

5
Taking Europe Seriously

In the spring of 1941, his passion stirred by the debate over Lend-Lease, Senator Arthur Vandenberg, then a leading isolationist, confided his worst fears to the privacy of his diary. "I hope I am wholly wrong," he wrote. But "we have torn up 150 years of traditional American foreign policy. We have tossed Washington's Farewell Address into the discard. We have thrown ourselves squarely into the power politics and the power wars of Europe, Asia and Africa. We have taken the first step upon a course from which we can never hereafter retreat."[1] Vandenberg was not wrong. A few months later the United States entered the European conflict, and victory in war four years later did not end the U.S. involvement. In 1945, no less than in 1941, American power was too decisive, and its influence too formidable, to be kept out of Europe; and Europe remained too important to America's interest, and too relevant to its history, to be abandoned to the hegemonic ambitions of any hostile power.

In the twentieth century America's ability and willingness to help the countries of Europe balance the rise of unchecked power in Germany and Russia have determined the conditions of war and peace in Europe: what to do with Germany, but also what to do with Russia; what to do with Russia, but also what to do with Germany? Between these two countries the primary cause for security concern changed, but they both remained central to security concerns in and about Europe.

In 1917, with imperial Germany about to defeat an exhausted France and a traumatized Russia, America's first of three successive rescues of Europe served the United States well, politically and economically—even if, admittedly, America's intervention was not necessary to save the country from a direct physical threat. Yet, once victorious, the United States lost little time in abandoning the Continent to its fate, especially since, in any case, its wartime allies showed less interest in President Wilson's principles for organizing peace than in his principles for waging war. Accordingly, Europe's democracies lost the peace as certainly as they would have lost the war had America refused to fight it. Two decades after the punishing peace treaty imposed at Versailles in 1919, Germany was on the march again.

This renewed challenge to the European balance was complicated by another land mass, the Soviet Union, which was born out of the defeat suffered by Russia in World War I. As Hitler's bid for hegemony was joined by Stalin's in 1939, each leader was willing to acquiesce temporarily to the other's ambitions in order to satisfy his own permanently. However united Europe's democracies might pretend to be or ever become, they could not resist the combined resources of two countries that had grown too big and powerful for a continent that had become too small and unbalanced. In 1939 World War II grew logically out of the failure to end World War I collectively—that is, to sign a peace treaty with, and not merely against, defeated adversaries, as had been done after the Napoleonic wars in 1815. After 1945 the Cold War, too, grew logically out of the Western democracies' inability to win World War II unilaterally—that is, without a Grand Alliance between all of them (including the United States) and at least one of Europe's two major totalitarian states (namely, the USSR) against the other. Whether settlement of the Cold War will permit a more lasting outcome than that produced by either world war remains to be seen. Room must still be made in the European space to accommodate countries that live in it as well as the many neighbors that still want to move in.

Making Europe Safe with Americans

With the end of the Cold War, it is tempting to celebrate victory as the result of enlightened policies devised long ago by American statesmen who knew what they wanted and acted accordingly, buoyed by the spontaneous and united support of their people. These heroic leaders, it is frequently asserted, had a "vision" of the world that helped them build an "architecture" for Europe. The enemy, it is remembered, had a threatening presence that could be understood simply and that needed to be defeated finally. The countries of Europe had a history that had been shared by the American republic long enough to be embraced in the name of compatible values and principles. Moreover, the nation had an abundance of power, relative to its own needs as well as relative to the power and the needs of others, that could be used as effectively to contain an identifiable enemy as to support congenial allies.

In this context, it is recalled, the policies that won the Cold War emerged quickly: in fifteen glorious weeks in 1947, when a new Democratic president articulated a doctrine that received bipartisan support from a Republican-controlled Congress, and in the two short years that followed, when the Truman administration laid the foundation for an architecture that included a European Community strengthened by generous U.S. economic assistance, and a North Atlantic Treaty Organization managed by superior U.S. military power.

However comforting such a reconstruction of the past may be, it is distorted. As a declaratory policy, Truman's clarion call to Congress on March 12, 1947, was deliberately dramatized to preempt partisan demands that Roosevelt's "appeasement" of the Soviet Union be ended. Truman's declaration that "we must assist free peoples to work out their own destinies in their own way" was not a doctrine but sales hype pressed on the Democratic president by the 1946 congressional elections, which had installed a Republican majority in Congress. During the war years, President Roosevelt's management of U.S.-Soviet relations could not become a partisan issue. But Roosevelt was now dead, the war was over, the Grand

Alliance was defunct, and Truman was an easy target. He was, complained Governor Thomas Dewey, a "captive of left-wing splinter groups," a characterization that some of the president's more adamant critics would have found too generous.[2] Accordingly, in early 1947, an embattled president found it necessary to tell his political rivals at home what they wanted to hear about the world, which they had made most explicit. But he remained unable to tell enemies abroad what the nation was ready to do in the world. Truman himself still tended to "look one way, and go another," as Henry Wallace complained in October 1945, and as Truman continued to do in 1948 after he had presented his doctrine to the nation.[3]

Saying one thing and doing another was a symptom of more than only the administration's confusion. Throughout the country considerable doubts lingered as to the true nature of the Soviet threat to the American republic and the desirability of America's continued involvement in world affairs. There was no Cold War in the spring of 1947, or at least not yet. Although the competition for power and influence between the United States and the Soviet Union was all too evident, Soviet intentions still seemed uncertain. During the war, exaggerated praises about Soviet contributions to the war effort had been common: praises about its people, who fought side by side with Americans, and about its leader, whose magnetic personality was occasionally exalted as a main asset for the Grand Alliance.[4] After the war, an orgy of good feelings found its way in the streets of Moscow, where spontaneous demonstrations of frantic friendship fed hopes that the Grand Alliance might outlast the end of the war.[5] From within, wrote Truman in his memoirs, the United States "was . . . flooded with isolationist propaganda under various guises, and many of us were apprehensive lest the isolationist spirit again become an important political factor."[6] John Quincy Adams's warning against Europe's "wars of interest and intrigue, of individual avarice, envy and ambitions" still held sway in a country that would have welcomed the same kind of comprehensive and swift retrenchment as had been achieved after the previous war.

That America's break with its isolationist past would have been engineered by Truman is not without some irony; there seemed to be little in the president's background that prepared him for this historic role, and little evidence of the character he would demonstrate in later years while steering the country into Europe and through the maelstrom of the Cold War. Ignored during the 1944 presidential campaign by an incumbent who had no time to meet with him, and who showed no interest in joint campaign appearances, Truman was forgotten in the months that followed the election in November and the inauguration in January 1945. On the day of Roosevelt's death Senator Vandenberg, who had briefly considered a run for his party's presidential nomination in 1944, feared the new president's "limited capacities" as "the gravest question-mark in every American heart." His conclusion that Truman could "swing the job" was reached hesitantly.[7]

"The cult of mediocrity," wrote Walter Lippmann in January 1946 in a direct allusion to Truman, "is not democracy. It is one of the diseases of democracy."[8] Two years later, after his grand vision for the world had been outlined, Truman was still viewed skeptically on both sides of the political spectrum. Even his surprising election to a full presidential term in 1948 failed to signal the dramatic rise in popularity that awaited him. Instead, the communist victory in China, a country that Truman was charged to have lost, and the outbreak of hostilities in Korea, a war that he was said to have permitted, caused extraordinarily bitter partisan and increasingly personal attacks against him and his administration's "crazy assortment of collectivist cutthroat, crackpots and communist fellow traveling appeasers."[9]

After the two-year night of the long knives that lasted for the remainder of Truman's presidency, a newly elected Republican president denounced containment, the central feature of Truman's vision, as "non-moral." Instead, Eisenhower's first Inaugural Address promised a "new and positive foreign policy" that would "know and observe the difference between . . . a thoughtfully calculated goal and the spasmodic reaction to the stimulus of emergencies."[10] Europe, the central pillar of Truman's postwar architecture, was quickly threatened with a reappraisal of U.S. commitments in a tone suggesting that the reappraisal might not be as "agonizing" as

Secretary of State John Foster Dulles pretended. Yet, extended beyond Europe by the Eisenhower administration, the course laid out by Truman became so enlarged during the Kennedy and Johnson administrations that the principal intellectual father of containment later felt compelled to deny paternity of a strategy that, in George Kennan's judgment, had "lost much of its rationale [after] the death of Stalin [in March 1953] and with the development of the Soviet-Chinese conflict."[11]

In the end, a vision is no more than what is remembered after everything has worked, and the structure it establishes is what is left standing after everything has been rebuilt. Along the way, the vision serves, at best, as a flashlight that can shed some illumination on a bit of what lies ahead and a bit of what has been left behind, but little more. During the Cold War, Europe was kept safe by an American vision that carried Truman's name but depended for its application on his successors, who interpreted that vision as they saw fit in light of the convictions they held and the conditions they faced, at home no less than abroad.

NATO's place in Truman's vision was, of course, central to the development of U.S. policies toward Europe. As signed in April 1949, the North Atlantic Treaty was an old-fashioned alliance that few recognized as the entangling partnership it became. A loose and general declaration of intentions, its text did not place the United States at the mercy of the foreign policies of its allies.[12] Although its operative clause declared an armed attack against any member an attack against all, each member was left free to take, individually and with others, whatever action it deemed necessary in a manner that was fully compatible with its due constitutional process. More specifically, the 1949 treaty did not automatically commit the United States to war in the event of armed aggression against any part of the North Atlantic area narrowly defined at the explicit insistence of the United States.[13]

Nor did the treaty demand, or its signatories expect, a more or less permanent deployment of substantial numbers of U.S. ground forces in Europe.[14] Such a contribution was found neither necessary nor desirable while the treaty was being negotiated, when it was signed, and immediately after it was ratified. No large-scale military action by the Soviet Union against Western Europe was deemed likely. This was a view that prevailed in Europe before the Soviet coup in Czechoslovakia: "It seems unlikely that the Soviet Union is making plans to start a war with Great Britain or the United States," argued Britain's Foreign Secretary Bevin in early 1948.[15] It remained the prevailing view in the United States after the Soviet explosion of an atomic bomb in late 1949: "The Soviet Union does not now contemplate large-scale military aggression in Europe," noted John Foster Dulles, then a U.S. senator, in September 1949.[16]

Modestly enough, the North Atlantic Treaty was signed as a guarantee pact designed to deter aggression, whatever its origin, by providing Europe with the decisive message that, in contrast with what had occurred in 1914 and 1939, there could be no war without early and even massive U.S. participation. This is the message European democracies had hoped to hear from the United States in 1919, after a war they had won together. This is also the warning they had wanted Germany to hear in 1939, on the eve of a war they knew they would have to fight together. But the commitment thereby made by the United States to the defense of Europe was not designed to be open-ended. Instead, it aimed at giving the Europeans the encouragement they needed to attend to their own security needs—"in the shortest possible time" and at least for "the initial phases of external aggression," emphasized Truman in July 1949. Hence the treaty's explicit emphasis on self-help and mutual aid: Europe would be kept safe with American power until such time as it could be made safe by European power.

Like Europe in 1945, the Atlantic Alliance in 1950 was a house with a soft shell. The outbreak of the Korean War, by providing substance and urgency to a threat whose origin and methods had been previously displayed in Eastern Europe with the Czech coup in March 1948, changed once and for all any remaining perception that the Soviet threat was benign. Understood as the harbinger of things to come in Europe, especially Germany, the Soviet-sponsored attempt to unify Korea by force provided a convincing opportunity to adopt and implement urgently a policy recommended in private for many months before in the United States and Europe. "From now on," emphasized Acheson, "it is action which counts and not further resolutions or further plans or further meetings." Based on plans that had been prepared in 1948, a large and rapid buildup of U.S. and allied military strength was launched.[17] Calls for a tangible U.S. presence in Europe became irresistible. Arguing that Europe "could not act as a mercenary army or defensive outpost" for the United States, Bevin urged that "America must be prepared to come at once."[18] Otherwise, the French complained, there would be little left to liberate, except for the corpses of Europeans who died in battle. Arrangements for an integrated military structure followed. They added to the North Atlantic Treaty a wholly new and unforeseen dimension—the apparatus of a regional organization that became known as NATO.

In sum, the 1949 North Atlantic Treaty was a child of World War II. Each member of the alliance, from its own national vantage point, confronted a mix of threats that required the omnidirectional security guarantees provided by the treaty, against a victorious Soviet Union and a defeated Germany but also against domestic instabilities. But in 1950 NATO itself was a child of the Cold War. A logical corollary of the treaty after the outbreak of the Korean War, it was aimed explicitly at containing further Soviet advances, not only in Western Europe but, by implication, everywhere around the world. With this change of direction came the deployment of U.S. forces, West Germany's admission to, and rearmament in, both the treaty and the organization, and the application of extended deterrence. With this change also came the institutional paraphernalia that transformed the 1949 treaty into the integrated military structure it became in the 1950s—providing its members with the option, exercised first by France in 1966, to leave the organization but remain in the alliance.

Reduced to countering Soviet advances in Europe, containment might be too passive, however. In criticizing this apparent blinder placed on the Truman vision of security in Europe, Eisenhower was not wrong. The rollback of Soviet positions in the East was the natural outcome of containment. It was pledged by Dulles, who viewed the liberation of Eastern Europe as the ultimate objective of U.S. policy. Hindsight now shows that this objective was not as far-fetched as it was made to appear after all. Hindsight also reveals that Dulles's much maligned predictions of an impending collapse of the Soviet system provided a look at the future that should have been taken more seriously than it was. For forty years, the experts' failure was to dismiss any such future too soon. Yes, the Soviet Union was an "evil empire" that carried within itself the seeds of its own decay. Yes, throughout the Cold War, an American victory was within reach even when it was feared that at best the stalemate between the two superpowers would end with their mutual exhaustion or, at worst, with a war that neither side would ever be truly prepared to wage.

As the walls of the Soviet empire collapsed under the Jericho-like trumpeting of the Reagan administration, Truman would have been pleasantly surprised by the credit he received after four decades of much criticism. He, too, would have shared the experts' surprise at the events that unfolded in 1989 and thereafter. He would have marveled over the willingness of the American people, so anxious to return home after 1945, to sustain their commitment long enough to achieve the objectives he had outlined for the nation in 1947. Remembering the pressures he faced from the Right for an early confrontation with Stalin, Truman would have been astonished that four decades of Cold War did not produce any armed conflict between the two countries. Remembering the pressures he faced from the Left for an early Grand Bargain with Stalin, Truman would have wondered at how changes in U.S.-Soviet relations could have been as one-sided as they proved to be when the Cold War came to an end.

That Truman's vision alone suffices to explain why changes dismissed as "unthinkable" for so long became "inevitable" so quickly is doubtful. From Eisenhower, who carried the vision worldwide, to Kennedy, Johnson, Nixon, and Ford, who used force and waged war on its behalf, to Carter, who tried to escape its vicissitudes as a national birthright, to Reagan, who revived it as evidence of the nation's disdain for its adversary, and to Bush, who ended the confrontation in victory, each president relied on a vision he could legitimately call his own. Yet any one vision of the country's role in the world had to manage the troubled vocation of a people that shows little taste for empire and is more comfortable at home than it is abroad—as John Quincy Adams once put it, a country that its people want to see as "the well wisher to the freedom and independence of all, . . . the champion and vindicator only of her own."[19] It is this vocation that drove Truman's discourse as he brought the United States into an entangling alliance with the countries of Europe during the Cold War. And it is this vocation, too, that now threatens to drive the United States out of Europe after the Cold War—by declaring the threat over, bringing the troops home, and leaving Europe to itself, with the good conscience provided by a job done well and successfully.

Keeping Europe safe still requires America, however, and keeping America safe still requires Europe. These guidelines of U.S. policies toward the European continent did not grow out of the Cold War. The 1949 North Atlantic Treaty was not caused by the Cold War, whose sudden end, therefore, need not make it obsolete either. Then as now, this treaty remains the clearest and most credible indication of America's commitment to remaining a European power. Ending that commitment would imply that America no longer has interests in Europe worth defending or that any such interests, however defined, no longer appear threatened.

The absence of this commitment would result in a vacuum that could be filled best by Germany, the dominant state in Western Europe, and Russia, the logical heir of what used to be known as the Soviet Union, in Eastern Europe. Now as before, neither is acceptable to the other, and both are feared by their neighbors. But whereas Germany can be contained in the context of a European Community that dilutes its national sovereignty, Russia can still be contained only in the context of an Atlantic community that balances its military power. In short, so long as peace in Europe remains the condition of peace in the rest of the world, America will have an interest in stabilizing the Continent.

Keeping Europe Safe with Europeans

As World War II came to an end, making Europe safe called for two semipermanent objectives. The first of these objectives, which was kept covert, had to do with leaving Germany as a divided country unlikely to gain full sovereignty in either one of its two main parts. The other objective, which was soon made explicit, aimed at maintaining the Soviet Union as a pariah state forcefully separated from the Western part of the Continent. During the four decades of the Cold War, these objectives were fulfilled with unprecedented measures of integration. Economic integration in the European Community locked West Germany into a box over which it gained increasing influence but from which any escape became more difficult. Military integration in the Atlantic community brought the United States into Europe, where its power contained the Soviet Union, thereby condemning the USSR to live as an empire that brought neither security nor affluence to its many republics.

As the Cold War ends, the hope of keeping Europe safe remains tied to the respective fates of Germany and the Soviet Union. With regard to either or both, the *déjà vu* of the past resurrects old fears of military conflicts and political instabilities. Germany has lost its post-World War II divisions. But which Germany will it be: a "good" one, whose postwar commitment to democracy cures whatever instincts might have remained from its history as a unified nation, or a "bad" one, whose political stability might not endure the economic challenges of unification? The Soviet Union has regained its pre-World War I fragmentation. But what will become of its republics? United they were feared as a formidable military and ideological threat of unprecedented dimension. Divided they are feared as an economic burden and a political liability of unprecedented magnitude. Either way they can be neither included in, nor excluded from, any new European architecture, because of lingering memories of what the Soviet Union used to be or apprehensions over what it might become.

Thus the Cold War leaves Europe both steadfast and changing. East-West political divisions on the Continent are blurred, but its economic divisions are wider and more demanding. Germany is reunified, and thus potentially stronger. But without economic convergence between its former halves, political divergences are likely to grow, and the new German state may actually be more divided, and thus potentially less stable, than before. The threat of Soviet aggression is gone. But the remaining massive nuclear arsenal makes any prolonged civil unrest in and between the fifteen Soviet republics directly relevant to Western security.

As was the case with a defeated Germany after both world wars, the future of a defeated Soviet Union after the Cold War is assessed differently in the United States and Europe, as well as among the countries of Europe. The dislocation of the Soviet Union into its various republics, or its preservation as a union (minus the three Baltic states), can be legitimately advocated on grounds of self-interest in each established state in Europe and in the United States. But the nature and scope of military power still available to the Soviet Union or some of its republics, and the amount and extent of the resources required to rebuild its economy, are such that they leave either outcome, integration or disintegration, beyond the ability of the United States and its allies to influence decisively or manage directly.

These transatlantic and intra-European differences over the postwar treatment of a defeated state are not unlike those that prevailed over Germany after each world war. Nor do they change markedly the disagreements that shaped the allies' assessment of the Soviet threat during the Cold War. Unlike what is the case for the United States, the countries of Europe have lived longer with Russian nationalism than with Soviet communism. History, therefore, reminds them more forcefully than in the United States that they have usually felt safer with the latter, despite its military power and ideological appeal, than with the former, despite Russia's relative military and political weakness.

History also reminds the countries of Europe of their firsthand experience with the collapse of large empires, which belies those who would favor, anywhere, the benign dislocation of the Soviet Union. Territorial disorders of such magnitude cannot occur in an orderly manner. If anything, the painful events that accompanied the protracted disintegration of the Austro-Hungarian and Ottoman empires teach that Europe has found it difficult to live safely with small nationalities restored to the status of nation-states by the collapse of the empires into which they had been forcefully submerged. At issue is not whether these empires were legitimate, which they were not, or whether these nationalities had a legitimate claim at statehood, most of which had. But these empires at least prevented their subjects no less than their neighbors from making conflicting territorial claims of their own. As these claims threaten to be resurrected, the sunshine brought to the world by the peaceful revolutions of the past decade may yet prove to be a prelude to the storms that will follow in the decade to come.

In contrast with the Cold War period, when phases of East-West accommodation were greeted with more enthusiasm and even exuberance in Europe than in the United States, Europe's rhetoric about the end of the Cold War has remained generally more subdued and even more apprehensive than the United States'. Where else is an explanation of this ambivalence to be found than in the unfinished status of "Europe"? The new thinking that prevails in the West (over the role of the nation-state) and in the East (over the final demise of communism) helps engender the promise of ending in peace a century of total wars, which also happens to coincide with the end of a millennium of wars waged with increasing violence. But lurking in the future remain the threats raised by the realities of the past, in the East (a weak and divided Russia) as well as in the West (a strong and united Germany).

The resulting pattern of political dialogue among Europeans is not new either: not that between France and Germany, whose agreement may overcome, more readily than ever before, the historical fear that the former continues to show toward the latter; nor that between Britain and France, whose entente may be sought anew as Germany's commitment to the European Community is debated in London and Paris with an intensity that has not been matched since the late 1940s; or the parley among all three states in response to pressures that would be exerted on Western Europe from

Eastern Europe and everywhere else. "Let us unite Europe," Prime Minister Macmillan reportedly offered de Gaulle in December 1962. "We are three men who can do it together: you, me, and Adenauer."[20] Fearful of the pace and the scope of change in both Western Europe and the Western Alliance, Britain evokes two larger European and Atlantic communities opened to all the countries of Eastern Europe. But the preconditions are hardly negligible: after democratic reforms have taken root and when their economies are sufficiently competitive to be capable of sustaining membership. Is the objective, then, to expand the European Community to the East—though, admittedly, in an indefinite and so uncertain future—or rather, to use expansion as an alibi for postponing a deepening of its institutions in the West? Is the objective to strengthen the Atlantic community in order to reassert the ties with the United States—or rather, to dilute the ties with the EC states?

These renewed intra-European discussions among Britain, France, and Germany overlap with a continued dialogue between the United States and the Soviet Union. The former deal directly with the new boundaries of permissible political change: chiefly, the fate of the nation-state in Europe, including its erosion in the West and, though in a different form and with a different historical context, in the East too. The latter deals directly with the new boundaries of mutual security throughout the Continent: the fate of a military balance that would end its past dependence on the countervailing deployment of U.S. and Soviet forces outside their borders.

To be sure, Moscow would prefer to move beyond the narrow boundaries of its relations with the United States and to reap the benefits of its new political legitimacy within the broader context of a common European house now inhabited by the twelve EC countries. Such calls, though, are heard skeptically, whether in national capitals or in Brussels. What is envisioned, at most, is a European village where the luxury condominium building owned by the EC countries is separate from other apartment buildings inhabited by other European countries with varying degrees of squalor, and even modernized with widely varying degrees of generosity and tolerance. In theory, every effort will be made to reduce these divisions in a comprehensive European economic and political space positioned in a world still regulated by a variety of other global organizations. To do otherwise, and above all keep the East separate and distinct from the West, might have consequences as costly as the errors made after the end of both World Wars.

In practice, however, the EC countries show much reluctance to bringing new occupants from the East into their Community, as the time is deemed premature, the means unavailable, and the consequences unclear. As for the Soviet Union, to whom could membership be offered: to the union collectively or to its republics separately? In all cases the EC's relations with its former adversaries are likely to involve the diverse forms of associate status developed with the Third World: a collective agreement with most countries in the region (similar to the Lomé Convention, first signed with forty-six countries in Africa, the Caribbean, and the Pacific in February 1975), completed by bilateral trade agreements negotiated separately and tediously for the indefinite period of transition that has characterized the prenegotiation phase of every state seeking membership in the Community since 1973.

At the beginning of the 1990s American calls for new institutional and consultative ties with "Europe"—both the European Council and the European Commission—and for some rethinking of the relationship between the European Community and NATO, are heard with some doubts and even resentment. These are different, though, than in 1962, when President Kennedy called for an integrated Atlantic community, or in 1973, when President Nixon called for a new Atlantic bargain. The doubts, then, had to do with European fears of an American political takeover of the Community that would end whatever remained of each ally's identity in a Europe already under the influence of U.S. economic interests. The ambiguities, then, had to do with the proposals themselves—as noted earlier, too specific where they should have been kept general (about Europe's contributions to America's postwar burdens in the East), and too general where more specificity would have been helpful (about America's contributions to Europe's new burdens in the South). Today, doubts relate to considerations of timing: yes, but not now. Ambiguities stem from questions of substance: yes, but not so much. What is being asked by and of each partner in the two communities is said to come too early and to amount to too much.

Since the Cold War America's dialogue with Europe has emerged as two parallel monologues, one about the need to save NATO and the other about the need to complete "Europe." Both are heard with the same misgivings, and even passion, as were entertained previously during periodic moments of détente in U.S.-Soviet relations. Now as then, a European identity is feared in the United States because of its impact on America's own identity as a European power, while the latter is feared in Europe because of an alleged penchant in the United States for a hegemonic leadership that might no longer be necessary or even desirable. These perceptions are manipulated in the intra-European dialogue accordingly: as cause for inaction and delay for countries that want to move Europe more slowly—allegedly in order to keep the United States in Europe—or as further justification for initiatives for countries that want to move faster—allegedly to prepare for a U.S. departure from Europe.

In the past the countries of Europe, including but not limited to France, often feared that the end of hostility between the two superpowers would take the form of an entente—in Europe's view, a condominium—in which the two states would share in the spoils of a victory achieved decades earlier. With the Soviet leaders fighting worsening circumstances of territorial disintegration, political fragmentation, and economic degradation at home, little credibility is left to such claims. On the contrary, in 1990 Soviet applause for international law and order during the Gulf crisis and acceptance of its ally's humiliation in the war that followed were prompted by hopes for economic rewards from the United States and other Western countries (as well as Japan), which would be called upon, therefore, to share with their senior partner the spoils of victory. In short, the roles have been reversed. The Soviet Union is not going to be part of any bilateral arrangement with the United States about, or at the expense of, Europe. It is now Western Europe that may be part of a condominium about, or at the expense of, the Soviet Union and its former dependencies in Eastern Europe.

The crisis launched by Iraq's invasion of Kuwait also raised questions about the post-Cold War order that echoed the questions posed by the North Korean invasion of South Korea in June 1950 for the post-World War II order in Europe. In 1991, as in 1950, the central feature of the war was not only the fact of aggression but the demonstration of America's will to defeat it. Obviously the demonstration in both instances proved convincing. In 1991 it entailed the most impressive and the most effective display of military force since the allied landings in Normandy in 1944. It suggested that domestic woes and public lassitude with the world would not prevent the United States from resorting to force if and when necessary.

This demonstration of American power gave hints of a new international order based on the only hegemon still in place after the Cold War. As in the past, such a prospect did not leave the states of Europe indifferent. The kind of bipolar world order unveiled against the Soviet Union and its allies during the Korean War, and enforced by the Eisenhower administration against the allies during the 1956 Suez crisis, provided little room for an autonomous European defense of its own interests. After Suez, the much-needed reconstruction of Atlantic relations took place around the Anglo-American special partnership but at the cost of European unity—at least to the extent that Suez worsened France's doubts about Britain's reliability as its central partner in Europe. In another crisis in the Middle East in 1973, a forceful reaction from the Nixon administration to Europe's reluctance to endorse U.S. policies in the region denied the relevance of a European identity for the preservation of Atlantic interests. After the crisis, transatlantic unity was also sought, but not truly regained, around a special partnership, this time between the United States and the Federal Republic, and again at the cost of European unity. At least for a time, such reaffirmation of U.S.-German ties weakened the Franco-German rapprochement that had been started earlier by President Pompidou and Chancellor Brandt, soon to be replaced by Giscard and Schmidt, respectively.

The cohesion achieved by the Alliance in response to Iraq's aggression in 1990 compared well with these earlier instances of transatlantic discord in the same region, and over comparable issues of principle, behind which stood more practical considerations of Arab oil and Soviet power. Yet the aftermath of the war proved surprisingly similar to what had taken place in 1956 and in 1973: a dual debate over Europe's place in the Atlantic community and over America's place in the European Community. That the need for a European identity on security issues was now based on the Western European Union should come as no surprise. Where else? In the 1980s it was this much-neglected organization that was used by EC countries to organize their support for U.S. policies during the latter phase of the war between Iran and Iraq as well as to coordinate their action in the Gulf War a few years later. But that the United States would seek to reaffirm the Atlantic personality of any such identity by insisting that the WEU be placed in the context of NATO should also come as no surprise. What else? Even in the absence of a Soviet threat in Europe, the Gulf War served as a forceful reminder that the Atlantic Alliance still deserves to be taken seriously too.

By definition, NATO can make room for the Western European Union, since all WEU members, including France, remain members of the North Atlantic Treaty. But, also by definition, there is room for the WEU outside of NATO, since the treaty's operative clause (namely, Article 5) remains confined to a limited geographic area that does not include regions of vital importance to the interests of WEU members. What is to be resolved now is hardly the compatibility and complementarity of these two defense institutions, one that has proven its effectiveness and must be preserved, and the other that is still experiencing the pains of birth and must be nurtured. What is to be resolved over time are three more practical questions that must be addressed successively and can be resolved in different forums: first, the expansion of the WEU (which does not yet include three of the twelve EC countries—Denmark, Greece, and Ireland); second, the coordination of membership between the EC and NATO (the latter of which includes two European countries that are not yet members of the EC—Norway and Turkey—but might be associated with the WEU while France's own ambivalent status in NATO is resolved); and third, but later, the consequences that a

European Community so expanded as to include such neutral states as Austria, Finland, Sweden, and Switzerland might have on NATO, to which these countries might also be associated but in ways that remain unclear pending NATO's structures and even missions.

The vision of a European alternative to any exclusive reliance on the American hegemon has always been entertained on both sides of the Atlantic. Self-help in the shortest possible time was urged by the European visionaries who launched the European Community at a time when American visionaries were also organizing the Atlantic community. "Europe," declared Jean Monnet in early 1948, "cannot long afford to remain almost exclusively dependent on . . . American strength for her security."[21] The time is now, not because the U.S. commitment to make its power available on behalf of its allies' security has ceased to be credible, but because, after the Cold War, it has ceased to be desirable.

All too often in the past, the predilection shown by the countries of Europe for doing no more than what they were compelled to do by circumstances, and less than what they might have done out of necessity, has found a convenient alibi in what their senior partner insisted on doing with, without, or in spite of them. This European attitude can only be indulged in the future by pretending that the significant changes that have taken place in each of the two superpowers and on the two sides of the European continent do not count for much after all: in other words, that, past the Cold War, the transatlantic order will barely differ from the order organized during the Cold War.

But this cannot be, of course. The anticipation of a world order managed fully by and from the United States is incompatible with the growing necessity of reducing an American burden that is being revalued, according to the nation's traditional preference, to place domestic priorities over international priorities. The years when the European Community could expect to be protected exclusively by others are now gone. Europe can no longer be kept safe without the Europeans themselves taking primary responsibility for their security.

Making Room Elsewhere

Over the years, America's relationship with a strong and uniting Europe has been ambivalent. What has been at issue is not the American commitment to the making of Europe. Based on the conviction that unity would give strength to the European allies, this commitment assumed that the allies' new strength, used on behalf of common interests, would relieve the United States from the defense burden it had assumed alone after World War II. At the same time, however, it was sensed that political unity and economic recovery among the European allies might also carry a price for the United States. It was the nagging fear that this price, however measured, might be so large as to undermine the American position in Europe that produced an undertone of ambivalence in the U.S. attitude.

A few weeks after the North Atlantic Treaty was signed in April 1949, Senator Vandenberg already showed fears of the consequences that the end of the Cold War and the recovery of Western Europe might have on U.S. economic interests and political leadership. "The Soviets know they have lost the cold war in Europe," mused Vandenberg in his diary. "As a result they are under great pressure to get East-West trade going again. . . . The economic stabilization of Western Europe (in particular of Western Germany) pours a flood of new competitive commodities into the world's markets. American producers find themselves menaced in much of our essential export trade. It seems completely clear that we are winning the cold war while we are losing the long-range economic war."[22] While claiming victory in the Cold War was clearly premature in the summer of 1949, bemoaning or predicting defeat in an economic war with Europe was simply wrong. The Common Market, which raised the level of U.S. apprehensions in the economic realm even as the Cold War was heating up, hardly produced a European fortress. On the contrary, it opened the door to a U.S. corporate presence in Europe worth more than $150 billion by 1990.

As the Common Market was organized, the United States' competitive edge was reinforced by a cultural predisposition to redeploy its assets aggressively across national boundaries. In other words, U.S. firms, unlike their European competitors, did not wait for 1992 to treat Europe as one market. Instead, their subsidiaries in Europe quickly integrated their operations through a network of plants and infrastructures designed to increase and diversify their cross-border activities. Thus made operational on a continent-wide basis, U.S. multinationals acquired an identity that was often more European than that of their European competitors. Some of them might have been ostracized as they arrived on the European markets, most of them were welcomed when, after this initial implantation, they grew and prospered.

As the single market is organized, the major challenge these multinationals now face does not come, therefore, from a community in which they already have deep roots and with which they have worked closely and effectively in the past. Nor, as the single market takes hold, are they showing any diminished interest in a market that has become a main source of earnings for many U.S. corporate leaders. In 1989 IBM earned more than two thirds of its net income in Europe; that same year, U.S. spending in cross-border mergers and acquisitions amounted to about $11 billion.[23] Instead, in Europe as elsewhere, the major challenge to U.S. corporate interests has come from the opening of markets once dominated by the United States to new competitors, including those from Japan.

For many years, Japanese governments failed to give the Old World the same focused attention and meticulous long-term planning they gave the United States. In part, this attitude was influenced by Britain, Japan's closest partner in Europe since the end of World War II. In part, too, Japan confidently assumed that its interests in Europe would be protected by the United States, as was the case during the Kennedy Round of trade negotiations. Finally, the Japanese attitude paralleled the obsessive fear and hostility shown by most European countries toward them.

At any rate, whatever the reason, Japanese officials, as well as Japanese companies (especially those in the manufacturing sectors) now acknowledge that the European Community and its commercial opportunities were ignored for too long. Rather than a potential economic rival or partner, Europe was seen as an informal competitor for security, since the United States might become all the more weary of its allies in Asia as it grew weary of its commitment in Europe.

In recent years this reappraisal of Japan's ties to the Community has resulted from several factors, most of which preceded the implementation of the 1992 program. First, the restrictions imposed or sought by the U.S. Congress on Japanese imports and investments encouraged the discovery of "Europe" as a growing and dynamic market that might compensate for possible losses in an American market increasingly saturated with, and resentful of, Japanese goods and money. This is especially true of the car industry, which, in the face of a weakening of demand in many traditional world markets, is widely predicted to shift its main battlefield for market shares to the European continent. But new areas of triangular competition have appeared in many other vital sectors. In the aerospace industry, for example, the Far East has emerged as one of the fastest growing markets for commercial aircraft. There, the European consortium known as Airbus Industrie is likely to pursue an aggressive strategy aimed at entering a market heretofore reserved for U.S. aircraft makers.

These shifts are more than plausible. The devaluation of the Soviet threat reduces Japan's earlier dependence on the United States as the pivotal ally without which security would fade and instabilities grow. Initially encouraged by the memories of World War II, a teacher-to-disciple relationship of unequals between the two countries is no longer tenable after the Cold War. Japanese companies, in bringing to Europe their competence and resources, hope to escape the political trade-offs that are still imposed on their government by the United States. Accordingly, while EC action on dumping or demands on local content continue to produce tensions or worse, these deal generally with ways in which Japan does business abroad. They are viewed as regulations that can be negotiated more legitimately than "structural impediments" that restrict sales to Japan, which often have to do with the way Japanese live at home.

Similarly, the attitude of the Community, as well as that of its member-states and much of their respective business communities, toward foreign competitors has improved over the past few years. To be sure, apprehensions, and even mistrust, remain considerable. But these no longer exhibit the obsessive character displayed in earlier years, and tensions are easing. In some sectors doing business with—and specifically in—Japan has become a badge of honor, as if it were a conclusive demonstration of corporate effectiveness and dynamism, or as if it could be seen as a demonstration of newly achieved corporate autonomy from U.S. dominance. Japan's trade surplus with the EC countries grew steadily between 1984, when it amounted to $12.9 billion, and 1988, when it exceeded $30 billion. In 1989 and 1990 the decline in this balance, admittedly modest, revealed a faster increase in Japanese imports from more and more EC countries, as compared with earlier years, when the rate of Japanese exports increased markedly faster and Japanese imports came from a relatively small number of EC countries. Even though the ratio between EC direct investment in Japan (about $2.8 billion in 1989) and Japanese direct investment in the EC (about $41 billion) is still unsatisfactory, the growing inflow of direct Japanese investment in the Community is generally welcomed as an addition to the limited pool of available capital. The number of Japanese mergers and acquisitions in Europe almost doubled in the year to March 31, 1990, as compared with the previous twelve-month period. And beyond issues of trade and money, occasional Japanese calls for building a political partnership on a global basis with Europe are welcomed by the Community and its members, as they might permit the same juxtaposition of burden- and profit-sharing (through Japan's involvement in achieving stability in the Gulf or seeking recovery in Eastern Europe) as was sought over the years by the United States in its relations with its European allies.

Japan's new determination to increase its market shares throughout the European Community raises perhaps the most difficult challenge ever faced by U.S. subsidiaries in Europe. Going far beyond any one sector, it extends to most growth sectors at a time when America's own national champions might have hoped to compensate for slackening domestic demand and rising Japanese competition at home with their dominance of expanding markets in a shared European fortress. Consumer electronics is one instance of a leading sector that has seen a quick expansion of Japanese assembly plants in recent years. And, to add irony to a difficult situation that is turning worse, as the Commission opens the EC's doors wider, Japanese firms apply lessons learned from their difficult experiences in the United States, as well as from those taught by the early wave of U.S. corporate immigrants in Europe in the 1960s.

The car industry provides another example of Japanese competition in a market where U.S. manufacturers faced limited competition. This labor-intensive industry whose protection from Japan was, and remains, adamantly sought by national champions in France and Italy has been particularly contentious over the years. In the five years before the 1987 Single European Act, the Japanese market share increased more than twice as fast as the average yearly growth in new car registrations in Europe. Attempts to keep Japanese imports or transplants—that is, Japanese cars manufactured in EC plants— "voluntarily" limited to an arbitrary level of the single market, and for a period that might be as long as seven to ten years, would hardly leave carmakers in the United States indifferent, thereby contributing to an American and Japanese community of business interest against Europe. Yet efforts to bypass these barriers with direct Japanese investment in production facilities in Europe have ominous consequences for U.S. carmakers that settled in the Common Market many years ago—thereby contributing to a European and Japanese community of business interest against U.S. interests in countries where Japanese investments are welcomed or a European and American community of business interest in countries where these investments are still opposed.

From a U.S. standpoint it may be difficult to determine what is worse. Continued trade tensions between Europe and Japan would go against stated U.S. goals for a more open trade system, but they would preserve America's privileged role in the Community and, consequently, with Japan, too. Closer ties with a European Community that is struggling to arrive at a role and an identity going beyond its self-defined and self-serving economic rationale would serve U.S. political goals for a new world order well, but it would not necessarily serve U.S. economic interests as well.

The economic New Frontier opened in Eastern Europe by the Revolutions of 1989 is unlikely to provide a safety valve or outlet for these rivalries. On the contrary, it might open yet another front in the corporate war waged by American, European, and Japanese firms for market shares throughout Europe. Thus Italy's Fiat aims at compensating for sales lost to Japanese producers in the Community's single market by additional production and sales in the greater European economic space that extends to the countries of Eastern Europe, including the Soviet Union, where Fiat's well-established presence gives it a marked competitive advantage. Now, however, Fiat must face increased competition as the same motivation that has been driving its strategy over the years is adopted by American and Japanese carmakers that cannot remain indifferent to these new opportunities. Similar tensions are likely to emerge in any other growth sector in Eastern Europe: European resentment against non-European countries for their intrusion; U.S. and Japanese resentment against European countries for their protective instincts; and U.S. resentment against Japan for reaping, after the Cold War, the economic benefits of U.S. political sacrifices during the Cold War.

Yet the most difficult questions raised by the opening of Eastern Europe affect relations within the Community rather than relations between the Community and the rest of the world. The need to provide direct assistance and access to markets for the economic reconstruction of these countries conflicts with the necessity of attending to the needs of the poorer EC states. Whereas a measure of convergence in economic performance could be observed during the first fifteen years of the Common Market, when the national economies of the Six were relatively homogeneous, regional disparities have tended to increase since the 1973 enlargement from six to nine member-states. In the 1980s such disparities became even more apparent with the admission of Greece, Portugal, and Spain. Together with Ireland, these countries showed an average income per capita that amounted to 69 percent of the overall EC average in 1990, even though the rate of economic growth in Ireland, Portugal, and Spain outperformed the average EC rate almost every year from

1986 through 1990.[24] It was to attend to such discrepancies between and, in a few cases, within EC countries, that regional funds were increased by the heads of government in February 1988—as part of the SEA's commitment to strengthen economic and social cohesion in the Community.

In 1989 the EC's response to aid requests from Eastern Europe was facilitated by the unexpected affluence of the Commission's budget. With lower-than-expected expenditures on EC farm production and export support because of higher world prices, and with larger-than-expected revenues owing to vigorous economic growth, the Commission had money to spare, and the European Parliament promptly voted special aid packages for Poland and Hungary.[25] Predictably, the crunch came when these conditions were no longer met. The crunch will be worsened when monetary union takes away the ability of poorer countries to devalue in order to attend to their balance-of-payments difficulties. In sum, the competition for scarce development funds adds a further discordant note to the politics of state alignment within the Community. The competition could become especially fierce, as such funds might be made even more scarce by the de facto expansion of the Community to East Germany (whose gross national product per capita stands between that of Spain and Ireland), despite the Commission's claim that German reunification will cost the Community a modest $700 million a year between 1991 and 1993.

Nor is this all. Already unable to sustain a high level of direct assistance over time, the EC finds it difficult, even conceptually, to reorganize its economic space in a way that opens some room for more imports from Eastern Europe. With the collapse of the Soviet market for manufactured goods that remain generally unfit for Western consumption, the only compensatory markets available to producers in the East are in the European Community. These need to be made available with the same generosity with which U.S. markets were made available to the countries of Western Europe (and to Japan) after World War II. But although the political consequences in Western Europe of economic protection from Eastern Europe are significant, so are the consequences of doing away with any protection, especially in agriculture, where East Europeans are best equipped to compete effectively with their counterparts in the West. In 1991 the import regimes of Hungary and Poland were probably more liberal than that of the European Community. Paradoxically, closer trade relations between them and the EC are more likely to succeed if the former are made more protectionist rather than if an attempt is made to make the latter more liberal.

Thus, even as the Community struggles to define its geographic boundaries in Western Europe, the impact of international changes is felt in terms of increased calls from central and Eastern Europe on its resources, and in terms of increased competition from without the European Continent for market shares. How these new pressures are faced, and how the resulting tensions within the Community as well as between the Community and its partners in and out of Europe are resolved, will also affect significantly the terms and the pace of the continued transformation of the Community's institutions in other political and even military areas. After the revolutions of 1989 in Eastern Europe, of 1991 in the Soviet Union, and of 1992 in the European Community, the saga of European unification will still have many tales to be told, questions to be answered, and plots to be revealed.

6
Imagining Europe
After the Cold War

I magining how the institutions of "Europe" will develop during
the next decade is a daunting exercise. Over the years, those
who have followed the rise of "Europe" most closely, including
those who helped guide it most effectively, have simply acknowledged
the unpredictability of the road ahead. "I have never doubted," wrote
Jean Monnet at the close of his life, "that one day this process will
lead us to the United States of Europe; but I see no point in trying to
imagine today what political form it will take. . . . No one can say."[1]
No member of the Community can offer a political model of governance that would satisfy all other members. No precedent of community-building can be made fully relevant to Europe.

History often refers to the unification of Germany as an example
of economic integration that paved the way toward political union.
Such references are exaggerated. Neither the origin nor the nature and
ultimate consequences of the German *Zollverein* that followed the
Napoleonic Wars are comparable to the process under way in Western
Europe since the end of World War II.[2] At most, this example can be
used to observe that monetary union, which the *Zollverein* formed in
1857, can precede political union, which was achieved many years
later, following a civil war among the states of the German
Confederation and the first of three wars among the countries of
Europe. But there is little resemblance between the many German
principalities and free cities that entered into a customs union in 1834

by adopting the liberal tariffs of their dominant member, Prussia, and the few nation-states of Western Europe that began their quest for an "ever closer union" in 1957 with a common market that averaged the tariffs of its first six members.

Surveying the Continent as the Common Market completed its first decade, Carl Friedrich portrayed Europe as an emergent nation. "It is part of being clever nowadays to talk about the 'end' of European integration, about 'dead alleys,' 'crises,' and impending collapse," he wrote in response to an attitude that continues to this day. Yet, concluded Friedrich, "The realities [of the past ten years] tell a different tale."[3] And so, of course, do the realities that have emerged since. These realities show that the countries of Europe, every one of them, and Europe, all of it, have come a long way since their journey first began—a journey during which the elusive fiction of "Europe" has been transformed into the discernible presence of the European Community.

Democratic Deficit

Central to Europe's emergence as a living force is the European Commission, where more than ten thousand international public servants, not including an army of translators and interpreters, form an executive without a government, a government without a country, and a country without an identity. While the European Council that protects the interests of the nation-states quibbles, argues, and moans over all decisions, the Commission provides an executive machinery that attends to the business of the Community with increasing effectiveness, notwithstanding its dependence on the Council, which appoints the members of the Commission, and on Parliament, to which it was made technically accountable by the Single European Act.

Between each summit meeting of the European Council, held twice a year, lower-level meetings of the Council of Ministers, which take place about twice a week throughout the year, reinforce a habit of cooperation that transcends the nation-state. At these frequent meetings ministers from different countries get to know one another better than they know many of their colleagues at home. On issues over which they all share intimate knowledge, they gain a deeper appreciation of the problems faced by their counterparts in the Council. They also learn to work with members of the Commission, who often used to belong to the Council when they, too, were ministers in their national governments, and to which many of them still aspire to return in some capacity. A president of the Commission who hopes to be elected president of France, a prime minister of Holland who hopes to be appointed president of the Commission, and commissioners whose European responsibilities in Brussels follow or precede national responsibilities at home all move through a revolving door that links the European Community and its members. This, too, is a European reality that manages the rise of "Europe." It strengthens the fact of cooperation sustained by the Commission and with the Council of Ministers even when the appearance of confrontation is created by the European Council and from the national capitals.

The attention now given to the Commission—as compared, say, with the attention given to NATO's general secretariat—is evidence of its status. Reflective of the Community's economic clout, the Commission's president is increasingly viewed as an equal of other heads-of-state or heads-of-government. He is a significant participant in the Group of Seven, which is alternatively transformed into a group of three that treats "Europe" as the equal of North America and Japan, or a group of eight that accepts "Europe" as the equal of the other seven industrial powers included in the group. Other European groupings that were formed in opposition to the Community now seek admission, either individually or en bloc, in the course of negotiations over which the Commission (and, since 1987, the European Parliament too) also exerts significant influence.

The sources of the Commission's influence, and even authority, remain uncertain, however. Elected by no one, the Commission can claim no democratic legitimacy. Appointed by all, it projects no coherent identity. The Commission guards the Community's interests, which it pursues by initiating proposals and which it nurtures by implementing them. But there are few interests to protect unless the European Council, acting on behalf of the nation-states, has recognized them; there are few proposals to implement until the Council of Ministers, meeting on behalf of the European Council, has reviewed them; and there are few European laws to enforce until each national parliament, voting on behalf of its respective constituencies, has ratified them. The Commission's dilemma is to balance the European logic for a strong executive capable of addressing the problems faced by the member-states against the fragmented logic of nation-states anxious to preserve their sovereignty.

However challenged the nation-state may be in Brussels, it remains therefore, the dominant actor in Europe. Meetings of the European Council serve as an unquestionable reminder that it is the Community's supreme decision-making body. It is the Council that gives authority to the Commission, and not the other way around. Questions that are politically embarrassing or that cannot be resolved by any one state without its neighbors—questions that are related to the environment, for example—are conveniently delegated to the Commission. But responsibility for questions that might affect the nation's lifestyle and its priorities—questions that are related to taxes, for example—are protected adamantly. Community laws are made by the Council of Ministers, and the most significant among them are usually taken up by the European Council. Even though the right to secede may lack credibility, it is the ultimate proof that all members are in the Community by consent. In short, the nation-state loses nothing more on any one issue than what it is willing to relinquish at a given time.

Nonetheless, the Commission's direct influence on the member-states has grown steadily. With regard to some issues first, and now even with regard to a few of the EC's members, it is increasingly difficult to determine who is ruling over what and against whom. In early 1991, for instance, conditions attached to a three-year loan to Greece were so comprehensive as to represent a virtual takeover of its microeconomic policy. For that period, 1990-93, the Greek government was mandated to reduce inflation from 17 to 7 percent, cut its borrowing from 17 percent of the gross domestic product to 1.5 percent, reduce employment in the public sector by 10 percent, and broaden its tax base. To ease the appearance of Greece's subservience to the will of its partners, Prime Minister Constantine Mitsokatis quickly adopted these marching orders as if they were his own: "We told Brussels to tell us these things," he pretended.[4] But who was dictating to whom? As one of the three most recent EC members (with Spain and Portugal), as well as one of the three poorest (with Portugal and Ireland), Greece receives benefits from the EC budget that are approximately five times larger than its contribution. For Greece, as for its partners, life in the Community may not be easy, but life without it would be even more difficult.

Whatever the trade-offs may be, every new compromise toward greater integration reduces the ability of the member-states, rich and poor alike, to have their way in or out of the Community. No government can now claim to be pursuing domestic policies it can truly call its own. Extended over a ten-year period, the prospect first, and the fact next, of EC membership transformed Portugal as much as its revolution against a forty-six-year-old dictatorship. Started before 1986, an unprecedented inflow of foreign capital ushered in a period of economic expansion that ended half a century of lethargy and brought affluence to many of Portugal's citizens relative to others. Since 1986 the injection of significant funds from social, structural, and regional EC aid programs has helped modernize the nation's infrastructure and communication networks, opened its once-protected industry and its heavily subsidized agriculture, and improved its education policy and its training practices.

Elsewhere, the Community's hold over the French economy proved to be more credible than the vague promises that, if elected, France's socialists would somehow break with capitalism. The French government's agonizing reappraisal of 1982-83 was in part engineered by then-Finance Minister Jacques Delors, who was later appointed to the Commission and now contemplates a run for his country's presidency. Since the mid-1980s France's attitude toward foreign capital has become one of the most liberal in Europe. U.S. investments, always feared and often denied access in the 1960s, are welcomed in all industrial sectors. Notwithstanding the bellicose rhetoric used by Prime Minister Edith Cresson after her appointment in early 1991, foreign capital, even from Japan, France's new *bête noire*, has become all the more indispensable, as the European Commission does not allow the French state to provide its leading industrial groups with the assistance they desperately seek.

The principle of qualified majority rule adopted by the Single European Act has transformed further the conditions of political governance within the European democracies. In effect, it means that the tightest and most explicit instructions given by a democratically elected parliament to the government can become irrelevant if a country's representatives are in the minority when decisions are made by the European Council. In such cases—which, admittedly, do not yet include the most significant issues governing the lives of countries—national parliaments may have less than an equal say with a multinational body that can not only challenge but also transcend their historical mandate.

The unexpected consequences of each decision, moreover, often reinforce this tendency. Thus the abolition of border checks that will result from the completion of the single market means that national policies on immigration, terrorism, crime, and drugs—all vital issues of law and order about which states have adopted widely different positions throughout their history—may become largely inconsequential. Similarly, European citizenship, which was accepted by the Twelve in December 1990, might not only permit EC citizens to vote in local municipal elections but also extend common diplomatic protection throughout the world, with foreign policy consequences that may go beyond the scope of the initial agreement.

That this transfer of authority from elected governments to an appointed technocracy would take place without direct consultation with the people, and without the transmission belt of a parliamentary body of community-wide representatives, raises questions of democratic legitimacy. For three decades the European Assembly was able to advise, complain, or even delay, but it could not act directly against the will of either the Commission or the Council. Even giving the Assembly the legitimacy of its name took twenty-five years of heated debates after the Assembly voted to call itself a parliament in March 1962. As stated in a European Parliament report on institutional reform, "If the EC was a state and applied to join the Community, it would be turned down on the grounds that it was not a democracy."[5]

Originally, the direct election of the European Parliament was designed to improve public awareness of Europe and reduce this institutional deficit. But neither the three elections held since 1979 nor the institutional reforms of the 1987 Single European Act have done much of either. In most EC countries all three elections turned on national concerns rather than on Europe-wide issues. If anything, they served as a general rehearsal for upcoming national elections. Electoral participation fell steadily, from a high of 62.5 percent in 1979, to 59 percent in 1984, to a low of 57.2 percent in 1989. That the European Parliament would have drafted the Union Treaty that inspired the Single European Act confirmed nevertheless the potential influence of the Community's only elected body. Significantly, however, the Parliament was not invited to participate in the negotiations that led to the Council's adoption of the act. Although the act gave Parliament some additional authority, it also confirmed how little European parliamentarians are allowed to do.

As it moves past 1992 and the organization of a single market, "Europe" shows, therefore, many of the basic attributes of an economic superpower without the institutions that would give it the political coherence and democratic legitimacy needed to exercise such status. The European Council and the Parliament still fear the growth of the Commission in, and even above, the Community. The Commission and the Parliament resent the control still kept by the Council over Community decisions. The Council and the Commission still block the Parliament's request for more influence over either of them. And the Council, the Commission, and the Parliament still show impatience with either the passivity or the intrusiveness of the Court of Justice.

To be sure, the Single European Act engineered some changes in the allocation of roles and responsibilities among these institutions. These, however, were not enough to bridge either the democratic gap between the Community and the populace in each nation-state or the gap between the Community's institutions and its achievements. Giving Parliament legislative powers comparable to those of the Council of Ministers and making the Commission responsible to Parliament will not come easily. Any such attempt will raise more problems than it can solve so long as the distribution of executive authority between the Commission and the Council has not been settled. But giving the Commission executive powers comparable to those of the European Council, and introducing into the Council a majority rule over all issues, is even more difficult.[6] Thus the impact of the Single European Act on the institutions of the Community is not due to any one reform it may have permitted. Instead, its most significant impact is that it ended at last the taboo against any such reform of the Rome Treaty. Given the nature of the European process, this means that more frequent and more significant alterations to the Community's institutions can now be expected in the future.

Uncertain Journey?

The European Community is more than a free trade area. Frontiers, over which the nations of Europe waged so many wars, have lost their past meaning. The threat of invasions no longer comes from soldiers but from civilians. Political systems have converged around a form of governance that relies on features that no one state follows all of the time but which all states now wish to adopt or can claim most of the time.[7] Cultural values and national standards, too, have escaped their former boundaries. The French and the Germans we used to know are no longer those we now know: the latter have absorbed some of the arrogance often attributed to the French, and the former have acquired some of the discipline usually associated with the Germans. To be sure, "Europe" remains a community of differences, disparities, and even contrasts: regarding the availability and fertility of land, the attitude and skills of labor, the facility and reliability of communications. It remains a mosaic where people who do not look alike, and do not speak the same language, do not think alike and do not view the world around them in a like fashion either. They still engage in passionate debates over their undeniably conflictual past and their uncertainly cooperative future. But somehow, these differences no longer carry the same connotation as before. Any of them is worth an argument. None of them is worth a war.

The initial purpose of the Community was to build an architecture that would be large enough and strong enough to bind Germany, whether divided or united, to the West—away, that is, from the East and Russia, whether Soviet or something else. This objective has been fulfilled: for the Germans no less than for their neighbors, there is no turning back. To claim that Europe is too small for a Germany that affluence and unification have made once again too strong and too large, or to rediscover in central and Eastern Europe a *Lebensraum* that an imperial Germany will find once again irresistible, is to express fears rooted in a past that no longer resonates with the realities of the present.

Germany's unification was not achieved because of action taken by its government on the basis of strong nationalist pressures from the people. Instead, what made it possible was largely that it was neither expected nor sought by the Germans themselves. Public opinion polls show that following many years of decline, German support for European integration increased as prospects for German unification rose in 1989. Whether from the grass roots or in response to the actions taken or declarations issued by Chancellor Kohl, there is no indication that changes in the East have encouraged Germany's search for a special way that asserts distance from, or seeks dominance over, its neighbors. If anything, there has been a decline in Germany's position relative to its main EC partners, as the German government faces the mounting economic and political costs required for the reconstruction of a vast region that is increasingly impatient with the pace of change needed to obviate the fact of its poverty. In short, after the Cold War, the new objective is not to lock Germany into the Community: this is an old objective that has been mostly fulfilled. The novel objective, instead, consists in identifying the Community's role in a new European and global structure that might provide for affluence, stability, and security for its members, neighbors, and associates.

The precedence given by the Community to economic issues over political issues, however, still denies, in most cases, the single political voice that is needed if Europe is to be heard more consistently and more convincingly. Nearly all the reforms launched by the Single Act were designed to facilitate the organization of an internal economic market. That the EC must still learn how to speak a common language in foreign and defense policy is all too clear. At the beginning of a new decade the many European voices that continue to be heard on security issues deny Europe the influence it has gained over economic issues. The refusal to take seriously such available machinery as the Western European Union parallels other refusals to take "Europe" seriously. Even more generally, it implies a reluctance to acknowledge the dynamics of a European process that is not, and never was, limited to economic issues.

The transformation of the Soviet threat in Europe and beyond facilitates a common European defense to the extent that it is no longer aimed at a Soviet military force that Europe alone could not expect to match, let alone surpass. There are no echoes of the debates of the 1950s, except for the tendency, *faute de mieux*, to resume the quest for collective defense around a Franco-German *pas de deux*. Nor are there any echoes of the debates of the 1960s, except for the tendency to misunderstand any such attempt as an attack against NATO. If the states of Western Europe need a common defense, it is not because of any general war that might still erupt on the Continent. Now, as before and for the foreseeable future, no war in Western Europe, and no military action launched in Eastern Europe by the countries of Western Europe, is conceivable without prior consultation with the United States. Therein lies NATO's role, however much the threats that it was designed to deter have been devalued—significantly in the case of a divided Soviet Union that can still frighten its neighbors, and totally in the case of a unified Germany that no longer threatens them.

The temptation to turn to out-of-area issues to uncover and define additional functions for NATO is not supported by the organization's history of discord over these issues. There is no reason to assume that the end of the Cold War means the end of political, economic, and strategic differences between the Western allies in the Third World. During the Cold War, these differences prevented the creation of any Western consensus on global issues. Instead, they were conducive to constant tensions, competition, and sheer rivalry between the two sides of the Atlantic. These differences have not been resolved.

That Europe's vision of the Third World would be different from that of the United States is not hard to comprehend, even if it remains apparently difficult to accept. Whatever may otherwise be pretended, the European empires were neither an accident nor an aberration—let alone the result of an acute fit of absentmindedness. Instead, European imperialism was a most logical effort to bypass the natural limitations imposed upon the European continent by geographic circumstances. These circumstances have not changed. The imperial military and political structures of the past may have been dissolved, and they may never be resurrected in their earlier form. But the web of organizations, treaties, and cooperation agreements that emanate from the Community is designed to ensure the privileged economic and political ties needed by a region whose ability to process raw materials, and resell them as finished goods, depends mostly on the supply and pricing of related imports from the Third World. On these issues, "Europe" will continue to find it easier to speak with one European voice than it would with one "Atlantic" voice. The Anglo-French military intervention that was aborted at Suez in 1956 is a model more relevant to the future of Europe than the U.S.-led intervention in the Gulf in 1990.

What is already upon us, therefore, is neither insignificant nor unknown. The present does not represent a break from the past. Even though their timing admittedly defied prediction, the changes that took place in the late 1980s were the outcome of policies that, we now know, were dismissed too readily, and of trends, we should have known, that were neglected too steadily. The many hidden secrets that have been revealed by these changes will shape that present for many years to come, notwithstanding the inevitable imponderables of the future. The focus of the Soviet threat has changed, from one of imperial expansion to one of imperial disintegration. Central and Eastern Europe have come out of the historically unnatural period of domestic tranquility imposed by Soviet power. The two Germanys have been reunited into one. The countries of Western Europe have gained unprecedented political stability, united in a European Community that is for real. Threats in the Third World have persisted, even though Soviet mischiefs in these crises have subsided. And the United States remains a European power, for although its relevance to European security may have been modified, this relevance has not disappeared.

Thus the parameters of European security emerge. Of necessity, security in Europe still carries an important, if different, military dimension. The less definable the security threat, the more flexible the instrument needed to defeat it. For four decades the threat was known, and it was a formidable one. It called for an intricate Western military organization with a clearly recognizable purpose and no less formidable capabilities. Now the threat is less well known. Soviet military power has lost the ideological drive that caused its growth and prompted its expansion, but that power remains plentiful and hence possibly dangerous. Memories of a dominant and brutal Germany no longer have the intensity or the relevance they once had, but such memories continue to linger throughout Europe. Economic and political insufficiencies in central Europe no longer show the potential for worldwide conflict they once showed, but their likely impact on the Continent remains significant.

In the face of these lingering uncertainties from within, the security of Europe still depends on a relationship with the United States best written in the North Atlantic Treaty. On both sides of the Atlantic the rationale for the treaty remains unchanged: namely, a guarantee pact aimed at any threat to the security of its signatories. How this guarantee can be translated into capabilities—whose and where—will have to be negotiated during the coming years, not only between former adversaries but also, and perhaps above all, among the allies in the context of the North Atlantic Treaty Organization with which France's old quarrel should finally end.

In this context, references to the Gaullist legacy need some perspective and many qualifications. That President Mitterrand would remain a committed Gaullist on issues related to NATO, or that Prime

Minister Thatcher may have been a committed Gaullist on issues related to "Europe," assumes too easily that de Gaulle himself would have remained a Gaullist by the late 1980s. Unlike Thatcher, de Gaulle would not have waged battle against Germany's unification, which he might have welcomed instead with more pressing calls for political unity in Europe, as Mitterrand did. But unlike Mitterrand, and like Thatcher, de Gaulle's likely concerns over the nature and the pace of change in the Soviet Union and its republics would probably have prompted renewed calls for cooperation with the United States in NATO—an organization that he fought in the 1960s when he found the Soviet threat devalued, of course, but one that he had welcomed in the early 1950s when he found that threat more dangerous.

An Atlantic Alliance where nation-states maintain their commitment to mutual security in Europe remains, therefore, an intrinsic part of any future security system. But outside the Atlantic area, and into the disrupted regions of the Third World, conflicts escape the realm of both the Atlantic Alliance and NATO. Policies can be coordinated, to be sure, whenever there is a commonality of interests. But no such commonality can be assumed as a given of transatlantic relations, no more now that the Cold War has ended than before when the Cold War was waged.

This is not all, however. Beyond the military dimension, security in Western Europe is mainly about political and economic systems, about their performance and their relationships.[8] For forty years the slow and tedious European "journey to an unknown destination" has led to a community of states that now stand midway between the normalcy of the nation-state and the novelty of supranationality. The journey is hardly over, of course; between each past step, no detour was ever ignored, and the same is likely to be the case for future steps too. But the Community's institutions—the Commission, the Council, and the Parliament—and its alphabetical array of achievements and projects—EEC and EC, SEA, EMU and ECU, EPC and WEU—give meaning and substance to spreading references to "the" Community as the second pillar of the new security system for Europe. And, in this case too, the form and scope of America's involvement with the Community, as distinct from its relations with each EC state, will have to be defined and refined during the coming years. Suffice it to suggest that even as some representation is defined for the European Community in the Atlantic community, some representation, too, will be required for the United States in the European Community.

Strong and United

To pretend that we can perceive in detail the course that lies ahead is to open the way for the gloom likely to follow Europe's inability to fulfill its own objectives and meet its own deadlines. Looming into the future, there remain many causes for concern. New political realignments among EC states may be encouraged by events in and out of Europe that would encourage the revival of radical movements in the member-states—including the political consequences of failure in the economic reconstruction of Germany's former communist half and new flows of immigrants from the newly liberated countries of Eastern Europe or those of North Africa. Beginning with Yugoslavia and the USSR in 1991, but also possibly in Czechoslovakia and elsewhere in Eastern Europe in later years, political turmoil and even territorial disintegration caused by a rebirth of nationalism could spill across boundaries. Economic crises, including a deep recession in the United States, would worsen conditions everywhere else, with consequences whose only predictability is that they would undermine stability in Europe, and, even more certainly, in the areas of the Third World that remain of vital importance to the countries of the Community.

In short, there are many reasons why EC members are likely to appear once again deadlocked, and the European process derailed, over issues that they had agreed to resolve before. Yet the process will still go on because no one objective and its related timetable can ever be understood as either a point of departure or a point of arrival. And so it is, of course, with the single market of 1992. In the context of time, 1992 grows out of the achievements recorded during the first thirty years of the Common Market. In the context of space, it serves as the basis for new and deeper initiatives in the monetary and political areas.

At any one time, Europe's catch-92 is to appear (and even pretend) to be both impotent and powerful, marginal and intrusive, growing and fading, in order to shed some of its weaknesses and gain even more strength. Cases reported in the daily press help make the point: Under pressure from the competition commissioner, Leon Brittan, an Englishman, the French government suspends its plans to inject nearly $320 million of capital into Thomson, the consumer and defense electronics group whose controlling shareholder is the French state, after carmaker Renault had agreed to reimburse much of the $2.5 billion of the debt write-offs it had received earlier from the French government under the pretense of capital injection. The Italian government is ordered by the European Court of Justice to recover more than $500 million it poured into carmaker Alfa Romeo in the mid-1980s before selling it to national champion Fiat. The government of Ireland is forced to abandon projects it was about to undertake in order to increase milk production. All EC states are required by the Commission to provide detailed information on the financing of state-owned manufacturing companies.

And so it goes, with every decision asserting more control over the state. Countries from all over the world send some of their best public servants to Brussels, with the rank of ambassador. From the United States, state governors, too, travel to Brussels, where they give key officials from the Community an attention they seem often reluctant to grant officials of their own federal government or their own elected representatives: in 1989 twenty-five U.S. states exported more than $1 billion to the EC, and EC direct investments exceeded $7.5 billion in thirteen states. Better yet, city mayors from EC states rush to Brussels to negotiate aid from the Commission, which now often insists that it will not discuss such matters with national governments alone.

This is what "Europe" is all about: rules and regulations that, once agreed, cannot be broken or circumvented easily; and markets that, once opened, cannot be closed. Every week the Commission dispatches hundreds of missions to the member-states, essentially to tell their interlocutors what they cannot do in light of what they had so painfully agreed to do. Every week, too, the Commission handles dozens of complaints that some EC law is being broken. Every week it gains a bit more life as it cajoles or threatens its innumerable interlocutors into taking some action that they might have chosen otherwise to ignore. The "Europeans" who attend to these tasks have little to do with the Europeanists who, forty years ago, launched the process that is now making these tasks possible and necessary. The distance from Jean Monnet and his vision to Jacques Delors and his plans is reflective of the distance that has been covered as the former's vision has become a growing reality. To manage that reality, the approach that is needed is more practical and more gradual than what was needed to present the vision. French presidents Vincent Auriol and François Mitterrand, Germany's foreign ministers Walter Hallstein and Hans-Dietrich Genscher, Italian prime ministers Alcide de Gasperi and Bettino Craxi—these, in truth, have been different leaders for a different Europe. Yet, memories of what was achieved by the former help give substance to the European attitudes and actions adopted and launched by the latter.

To the extent that the Community has come to influence the day-to-day life of its member-states, the sovereignty of the nation-state has been eroded by the rise of "Europe." Over the years the scope of what is forbidden has been so extended as to reduce significantly the range of what the member-states can do without causing an immediate reaction from the Community and its Commission in Brussels. This does not mean that it has now become impossible for each member to reverse these decisions if it so wishes. If a majority of voters in one country want one outcome, and a majority of governments in the Community prefer the opposite, the voters are likely to win, at least for a while. France and Britain are two states that joined the European Community thinking along these lines, and their warnings of an impending withdrawal delayed the Community more than once.

This is not a melting pot, it was observed many years ago; it is more like a bag of marbles.[9] Removing a marble from the bag has become more difficult, however. Advocating withdrawal is tantamount to political suicide for any one party or any one political leader or any one state that would dare contemplate it. The political blitzkrieg that toppled Margaret Thatcher in late 1990 is convincing evidence that attacking Brussels can now carry a heavy political price in the nations' capitals. Not seeking membership is tantamount to economic suicide for any European state that does not belong to the Community yet. In October 1991 the agreement between the European Community and the European Free Trade Association to create a nineteen-nation free trade zone across the Continent confirmed the overpowering logic of "Europe." In an economic area where national sovereignty and national frontiers are increasingly ignored, most of the EFTA countries have already learned to be governed by rules that they did not make. Appended to the treaty were the 1,500 Community laws adopted by EC countries over the past thirty-five years. In a political space relieved of any single conflict en bloc, neutral states can now contemplate entering the "ever closer union" to which they had objected in earlier years.

There is a "union of the nations of Europe," wrote Jean-Jacques Rousseau about 200 years ago. They "touch each other at so many points that no one of them can move without giving a jar to all the rest." But such union, Rousseau added, was "formed and maintained by nothing better than chance"—by geography, that is. Any change causes "inevitably . . . quarrels and dissensions," thereby leaving "those who belong to it worse than . . . if they formed no community at all."[10] After innumerable wars of conquest, wars of unification, and wars of self-preservation, the unfortunate and conflictual European community of chance that Rousseau bemoaned late in the eighteenth century is turning into the prosperous and cooperative community of choice that Monnet dared envision for the twenty-first century. Much remains to be achieved before this long journey is completed. But the distance that has already been traveled makes the distance that still lies ahead short in comparison.

Notes

Chapter 1: Europe-92 in Perspective

1. George F. Kennan, *Memoirs, 1925-1950* (Boston: Little, Brown, 1967), p. 455.
2. On the Franco-German agreement of September 1958, see Charles de Gaulle, *Mémoires d'espoir*, vol. 1, *Le renouveau, 1958-1962* (Paris: Librairie Plon, 1970), pp. 184-89. On de Gaulle and Adenauer, see Alfred Grosser, *French Foreign Policy Under de Gaulle* (Boston: Little, Brown, 1967), pp. 64-67.

Chapter 2: Remembering Europe During the Cold War

1. Jean Monnet, *Memoirs* (Garden City, N.Y.: Doubleday, 1978), pp. 272-73. Robert Marjolin, *Memoirs, 1911-1986* (London: Weidenfeld and Nicolson, 1989) pp. 270-71. See also R.A.C. Parker, "British Perceptions of Power: Europe Between the Superpowers," and Pierre Melandri and Maurice Vaïsse, "France: From Powerlessness to the Search for Influence," in Josef Becker and Franz Knipping, eds., *Power in Europe? Great Britain, France, Italy, and Germany in a Postwar World, 1945-1950* (New York: Walter de Gruyter, 1986), pp. 447-74.
2. Anton de Porte, *De Gaulle's Foreign Policy, 1944-1946* (Cambridge, Mass.: Harvard University Press, 1968), pp. 74-80.
3. James F. Byrnes, *Speaking Frankly* (New York: Harper & Brothers, 1947), pp. 24-25.
4. Gustave Flaubert's *Sentimental Education* is quoted in Philip Green and Michael Walzer, eds., *The Political Imagination in Literature*, (New York: The Free Press, 1969), p. 409.
5. Simon Serfaty, *France, de Gaulle, & Europe: The Policy of the Fourth and Fifth Republics Toward the Continent* (Baltimore, Md.: Johns Hopkins Press, 1968), pp. 8 ff.
6. Paul-Henry Spaak, *The Continuing Battle: Memoirs of a European* (Boston: Little, Brown, 1971), p. 224.
7. Alfred Grosser, *The Western Alliance: European-American Relations Since 1945* (New York: Continuum, 1980), p. 81.
8. See Gordon A. Craig, "Germany and NATO: The Rearmament Debate, 1950-1958," in Klaus Knorr, ed., *NATO and American Security* (Princeton, N.J.: Princeton University Press, 1959), p. 248.
9. William E. Paterson, *The SPD and European Integration* (Westmead: Saxon House, 1974), pp. 64-66, 76-77, and 105, and Lewis J. Edinger, *Kurt Schumacher: A Study in Personality and Political Behavior* (Stanford, Calif.: Stanford University Press, 1965), p. 233.
10. Dean Acheson, *Sketches from the Life of Men I Have Known* (New York: Harper and Row, 1959), p. 171, and *Present at the Creation: My Years at the State Department* (New York: W.W. Norton, 1969), pp. 361-62.

11. Marjolin, *Memoirs, 1911-1986*, p. 278.
12. Charles de Gaulle, *Salvation, 1944-1946* (London: Weidenfeld and Nicolson, 1959), p. 59. Vincent Auriol, *Journal du septennat, 1947* (Paris: Librairie Armand Colin, 1970), p. 799.
13. Harry S Truman, *Memoirs*, vol. 1, *Year of Decisions* (Garden City, N.Y.: Doubleday, 1955), pp. 50, 78, and 412.
14. Arnold M. Rose, "Anti-Americanism in France," *Antioch Review*, December 1952, pp. 468-84; T.R. Fyvel, "Realities Behind British 'Anti-Americanism'—The Minority Leading the National Pastime," *Commentary*, December 1952, pp. 555-62; William G. Carleton, "An Atlantic Curtain?" *The American Scholar*, Summer 1953, pp. 265-79; and Norbert Muhlen, "German Anti-Americanism: East & West Zones," *Commentary*, February 1953, pp. 121-30.
15. Antonio Varsori, "De Gasperi, Nenni, Sforza and their Role in Post-War Italian Foreign Policy," in Becker and Knipping, eds., *Power in Europe?* p. 113. Grosser, *The Western Alliance*, p. 129.
16. Simon Serfaty, "An International Anomaly: The United States and the Italian Communist Parties in France and in Italy, 1945-1947," *Studies in Comparative Communism*, Spring/Summer 1975, pp. 123-47.
17. Quoted in C.J. Bartlett, *The Long Retreat: A Short History of British Defense Policy, 1945-1970* (London: Macmillan, 1972), pp. 1-2. See also, Max Beloff, *The Future of British Foreign Policy* (New York: Taplinger, 1969), p. 2.
18. Pascal Ory, "Introduction to an Era of Doubt. Cultural Reflections of French Power, around the year 1948," in Becker and Knipping, eds., *Power in Europe?* p. 400.
19. Quoted in Geoffrey Warner, "Britain and Europe in 1948: The View from the Cabinet, " in Becker and Knipping, eds., *Power in Europe?* p. 33.
20. George Lichtheim, "Europe's Democracy and American Imperialism," *Commentary*, January 1949, pp. 1-7.
21. C.M. Woodhouse, "Attitudes of NATO Countries Toward the United States," *World Politics*, January 1958, pp. 216-17.
22. Dwight D. Eisenhower, *Waging Peace* (Garden City, N.Y.: Doubleday, 1965), pp. 93-98.
23. See Anthony Nutting, *No End of a Lesson: The Story of Suez* (London: Constable, 1967), p. 37; Chester L. Cooper, *The Lion's Last Roar: Suez, 1956* (New York: Harper & Row, 1978), p. 191.
24. Singled out as the chief architect of this betrayal, John Foster Dulles was subjected to unprecedented criticism. One year after Suez, it was still written that "not since Hitler has any foreigner been so scorned and disliked in Britain." "Mr. Macmillan On Stage," *Economist*, October 26, 1957, p. 308.
25. Eisenhower, *Waging Peace*, p. 90. Donald Neff, *Warriors at Suez* (New York: Linden Press, 1981), p. 412.
26. Gerald Freund, *Germany Between Two Worlds* (New York: Harper & Row, 1961), p. 115.
27. Arnold Wolfers, "Integration in the West: The Conflict of Perspectives," in Francis O. Wilcox and H. Field Haviland, Jr., eds., *The Atlantic Community: Progress and Prospects* (New York: Praeger, 1963), p. 235.
28. Kennan, *Memoirs, 1925-1950*, p. 452.
29. William Clayton, "GATT, the Marshall Plan and OECD," *Political Science Quarterly*, December 1983, pp. 493-503.
30. See Michael Balfour, *West Germany: A Contemporary History* (New York: St. Martin's Press, 1982), pp. 143-52; Karl Hardach, *The Political Economy of Germany in the Twentieth Century* (Berkeley: University of California Press, 1980), pp. 161-92; and Henry M. Pachter,

Modern Germany: A Social, Cultural, and Political History (Boulder, Colo.: Westview Press, 1978), pp. 323-32.

31. At Rambouillet, remembered de Gaulle, Macmillan endorsed the French nuclear force. "We also have ours, [Macmillan said,] and we ought to be able to unite the two within a context that would be independent from the United States." But at Nassau, added de Gaulle, "Great Britain gave the United States whatever poor atomic forces she had. She therefore made her choice." Not surprisingly, Macmillan's recollection of this meeting is different. "The General was in no doubt as to my intentions . . . , that if the United States . . . cancelled Skybolt I would try to obtain Polaris in its place." André Passeron, *De Gaulle parle, 1962-1966* (Paris: Fayard, 1966), pp. 199 and 207. Harold Macmillan, *At the End of the Day, 1961-1963* (New York: Harper & Row, 1973), p. 348.

32. John Pinder, "European Community and Nation-State: A Case for a New Federalism?" *International Affairs*, Winter 1985-86, pp. 43-45.

33. Monnet, *Memoirs*, p. 494. Marjolin, *Memoirs, 1911-1986*, p. 346.

34. France's share of world markets grew after 1973 because of the strong French performance in the oil-exporting countries. But in the 1980s reduced demand in these markets was not compensated in such dynamic sectors as automobiles and electronics, or in the new markets in Asia, thereby causing a drop in the French share of world markets, which amounted to 6.7 percent in 1986, as compared with 7.5 percent in 1973 and 8 percent in 1980.

35. Michael M. Harrison, *The Reluctant Ally: France and Atlantic Security* (Baltimore, Md.: Johns Hopkins Press, 1981), pp. 164-219. See also, Michael M. Harrison and Simon Serfaty, *A Socialist France and Western Security* (Washington, D.C.: Johns Hopkins Foreign Policy Institute, 1981), pp. 27-34.

36. See François Mitterrand, *Ici et maintenant* (Paris: Fayard, 1980).

37. Ernst Weinsfeld, "François Mitterrand: l'action extérieure," *Politique Etrangère*, Spring 1986, p. 131.

38. François Mitterrand, "The Future of Europe," *World Today*, March 1987, p. 41.

39. Quoted in Ernest Wistrich, *After 1992: The United States of Europe* (London: Routledge, 1991), p. 16.

40. News conference of May 15, 1962. Passeron, *De Gaulle parle, 1962-1966*, p. 256.

41. U.W. Kitzinger, *The Politics and Economics of European Integration: Britain, Europe, and the United States* (New York: Praeger, 1963), p. 122.

42. John Mander, *Great Britain or Little England?* (Boston: Houghton Mifflin, 1964), p. 199.

43. Henry Kissinger, *Years of Upheaval* (Boston: Little, Brown, 1982), pp. 137-51 and 173-74.

44. Lloyd Gardner, "Lyndon Johnson and de Gaulle," paper presented at the Conference on de Gaulle and the United States, Commemoration of the Centenary of de Gaulle's Birth (New York University, April 4-6, 1990).

Chapter 3: Sculpting a Community

1. De Gaulle is quoted in Edward A. Kolodziej, *French International Policy Under de Gaulle and Pompidou* (Ithaca, N.Y.: Cornell University Press, 1974), p. 243. See Simon Serfaty's "Defining Europe: Purpose Without Commitment?" in Michael T. Clark and Simon Serfaty eds., *New Thinking & Old Realities: America, Europe and Russia* (Washington, D.C.: Seven Locks Press, 1991), pp. 127-61.

2. Spaak, *The Continuing Battle*, p. 195.

3. Quoted in Richard Mayne, *The Recovery of Europe* (New York: Harper & Row, 1970), p. 169.

4. Michael Curtis, *Western European Integration* (New York: Harper & Row, 1965), p. 34.
5. Monnet, *Memoirs*, p. 303. In the 1950s the impact of the ECSC on the coal and steel industry of the six member-states was relatively limited. See William Diebold, Jr., *The Schuman Plan* (New York: Praeger, 1959).
6. Harry S Truman, *Memoirs*, vol. II, *Years of Trial and Hope, 1946-1952* (Garden City, N.Y.: Doubleday, 1956), p. 413.
7. Robert McGeehan, *The German Rearmament Question: American Diplomacy and European Defense After World War II* (Chicago: University of Illinois Press, 1971), pp. 236-38.
8. Quoted in Richard Rosecrance, *Defense of the Realm: British Strategy in the Nuclear Epoch* (New York: Columbia University Press, 1968), p. 147.
9. Simon Serfaty, *American Foreign Policy in a Hostile World: Dangerous Years* (New York: Praeger, 1984), p. 200.
10. Monnet, *Memoirs*, p. 403.
11. Sidney Dell, *Trade Blocs and Common Markets* (New York: Knopf, 1963), p. 108.
12. Kitzinger, *The Politics and Economics of European Integration*, p. 18.
13. Serfaty, *France, de Gaulle and Europe*, p. 66.
14. R.L. Mowat, *Creating the European Community* (New York: Harper & Row, 1973), p. 145.
15. Paul Reynaud, *The Foreign Policy of Charles De Gaulle* (New York: Odyssey Press, 1964), p. 51.
16. The advantages of a decline in Britain's influence in and over the United States were discussed in Germany as early as 1949. See Dell, *Trade Blocs and Common Markets*, p. 125.
17. Roger Morgan, "The Historical Background, 1955-85," in Roger Morgan and Carolyn Bray, eds., *Partners and Rivals in Western Europe: Britain, France and Germany* (Aldershot, Hants: Gower Publishing Company, 1986), p. 11. Wolfram Hanrieder, *West German Foreign Policy, 1948-1963* (Stanford, Calif.: Stanford University Press, 1967), p. 165.
18. Harold Macmillan, *Pointing the Way, 1959-1961* (New York: Harper & Row, 1972), p. 350-51. After the initial tariff cutting of January 1959, the Six quickly offered tariff cuts to nonmembers. Herbert G. Nicholas, *Britain and the U.S.A.* (Baltimore, Md.: Johns Hopkins Press, 1963), p. 150.
19. Ernest Preeg, *Traders and Diplomats* (Washington, D.C.: Brookings Institution, 1970), pp. 285-86.
20. George Lichtheim, *Europe and America: The Future of the Atlantic Community* (London: Thames and Hudson, 1963), p. 151.
21. David P. Calleo, *Britain's Future* (New York: Horizon Press, 1968), pp. 18-19.
22. Eisenhower, *Waging Peace*, p. 604. Arthur M. Schlesinger, Jr., *A Thousand Days: John F. Kennedy in the White House* (Boston: Houghton Mifflin, 1965), pp. 654-55.
23. The system worked in reverse for exports: the EC paid an exporter the difference between the high internal target price and the lower world market price. Dell, *Trade Blocs and Common Markets*, p. 150.
24. See Graham Avery, "Agricultural Policy and American Comparisons," *European Affairs*, Spring 1987, pp. 62-74, and Gisela Hendriks, "Germany and the CAP: National Interests and the European Community," *European Affairs*, Winter 1989, pp. 75-87.
25. Joan Edelman Spero, *The Politics of International Economic Relations* (New York: St. Martin's Press, 1977), p. 86.
26. Curtis, *Western European Integration*, p. 214.
27. Karl Hardach, *The Political Economy of West Germany in the Twentieth Century*, pp. 186-92.

28. F. Roy Willis, *Italy Chooses Europe* (New York: Oxford University Press, 1971), pp. 294-295. Wistrich, *After 1992*, p. 3. Calleo, *Britain's Future*, p. 20.

29.
Intra-EC Trade in Percentage of Member-States' Total Exports

	1958	1970
Belg/Lux	55.4	75.2
France	30.9	58.1
Germany	37.9	49.8
Italy	34.5	51.7
Netherlands	58.3	72.6

30. Fred L. Block, *The Origins of International Economic Disorder* (Berkeley: University of California Press, 1977), p. 145. Spero, *The Politics of International Economic Relations*, p. 73.
31. Robert E. Hudec, *The GATT Legal System and World Trade Diplomacy* (New York: Praeger, 1975).
32. Spero, *The Politics of International Economic Relations*, p. 106.
33. David P. Calleo and Benjamin Rowland, *America and the World Economy* (Bloomington: Indiana University Press, 1973), pp. 166-67 and 316.
34. Gary Clyde Hufbauer, "Europe 1992: Opportunities and Challenge," *Brookings Review*, Summer 1990, p. 14.
35. David Lerner, "Reflections on France in the World Arena," in Raymond Aron and D. Lerner eds., *France Defeats EDC* (New York: Praeger, 1957), p. 209.
36. Harrison, *The Reluctant Ally*, p. 104.
37. Kitzinger, *The Politics and Economics of European Integration*, p. 92; Maurice Couve de Murville, *Une politique étrangère, 1958-1969* (Paris: Plon, 1971), pp. 360-75.
38. De Gaulle, *Mémoires d'espoir*, p. 195. See also, R.C. Mowat, *Creating the European Community*, pp. 178-88.
39. Peter Coffey, *The European Monetary System—Past, Present and Future* (Dordrecht: Kluwer Academic Publishers, 1987), p. 6.
40. Stanley Hoffmann, "No Trumps, No Luck, No Will: Gloomy Thoughts on Europe's Plight," in James Chace and Earl Ravenal, eds., *Atlantic Lost: U.S.-European Relations after the Cold War* (New York: New York University Press, 1976), pp. 1-46; Walter Laqueur, "The Idea of Europe Runs Out of Gas," *Atlantic Community Quarterly*, Spring 1974, pp. 64-75.
41. Roger Morgan, "The Federal Republic of Germany," in Carol and Kenneth J. Twitchett, *Building Europe: Britain's Partners in the EEC* (London: European Publications Limited, 1981), p. 67.
42. Monnet, *Memoirs*, p. 513. Schmidt became chancellor on May 14, 1974, and Giscard was elected president a few days later.
43. David P. Calleo, *Beyond American Hegemony: The Future of the Western Alliance* (New York: Basic Books, 1987), p. 96.
44. See Peter Ludlow, *The Politics and Diplomatic Origins of the European Monetary System, July 1977-March 1979*, The Johns Hopkins Bologna Center, Occasional Papers, No. 32 (June 1980).
45. Samuel Brittan, "Why ERM needs monetary union," *Financial Times*, October 25, 1990.
46. Tom de Vries, "On the Meaning and Future of the European Monetary System," *Essays in International Finance*, Princeton University, September 1980, pp. 16-21.

47.

Currency Realignments in the EMS, 1979-1984

	9/24/79	11/30/79	3/23/81	10/5/81	2/22/82	6/14/82	3/21/83
Belg/Lux					-8.50		+1.5
Denmark	-2.9	-4.8			-3.00		+2.5
France				-3.0		-5.75	-2.5
FRG	+2.5			+5.5	+4.25	+5.50	
Holland				+5.5		+4.25	+3.5
Ireland							-3.5
Italy			-6.0	-3.0		-2.75	-2.5

See Manuel Guitián, "The European Monetary System: A Balance Between Rules and Discretion," in *Policy Coordination in the EMS*, IMF Occasional Papers (September 1988), p. 19. Also *Problèmes Economiques*, April 12, 1989, p. 21.

48. Helmut Schmidt, "The European Monetary System: Prospects for Further Progress," *World Today*, May 1985, p. 87. Albert Bressand, "Currency chaos: the newest strategic tool," *The International Economy*, October/November 1987, p. 46.

49.

Currency Realignments in the EMS, 1985-89

	7/22/85	4/7/86	8/4/86	1/12/87
Belg/Lux	+2.0	+1.0		+2.0
Denmark	+2.0	+1.0		
France	+2.0	-3.0		
FRG	+2.0	+3.0		+3.0
Holland	+2.0	+3.0		+3.0
Ireland	+2.0		-8.0	
Italy	-6.0			

Sources: Guitián, "The European Monetary Systems," p. 19, and *Problèmes Economiques*, April 12, 1989, p. 21.

50. Tomaso Padoa-Schioppa, "Public Policy and the EMS Experience," in W.H. Butler and R.M. Marston, eds., *International Economic Policy Coordination* (Cambridge, Mass.: Cambridge University Press, 1984), p. 89. See also Heinz-Dieter Smeets, "Does Germany Dominate the EMS?" *Journal of Common Market Studies*, September 1990, p. 37.

51. "Straighten Europe's Snake," *Economist*, June 3, 1989, p. 17.

52.

Unemployment Rates in Some EEC Countries

	1970	1973	1979	1981	1983	1984	1985	1986	1987	1988	1989	1990
Britain	3.0	3.0	5.0	9.8	12.5	11.7	11.2	11.2	10.3	8.5	7.1	6.9
France	2.5	2.7	5.8	7.4	8.3	9.7	10.2	10.4	10.5	10.0	9.4	9.0
Germany	0.7	0.9	3.1	4.5	8.0	7.1	7.2	6.4	6.2	6.2	5.6	5.1
Italy	5.3	6.3	7.6	7.8	9.3	9.3	9.6	10.4	10.9	10.9	10.9	9.8
U.S.	4.9	4.8	5.8	7.5	9.5	7.4	7.1	6.9	6.1	5.5	5.3	5.5

53. Michael Emerson, "1992 and Beyond: The Bicycle Theory Rides Again," *Political Quarterly*, July-September 1988, p. 293.
54. Frank McDonald and George Zis, "The European Monetary System," *Journal of Common Market Studies*, March 1989, p. 186.
55. Robert Triffin, "The International Monetary System and the European Monetary System," *EFTA Bulletin*, March 1987, p. 10.
56. Massimo Russo and Giuseppe Tullio, "Monetary Coordination Within the European Monetary System: Is There a Rule?" in *Policy Coordination in the EMS*, p. 47.
57. Anastasia Pardalis, "European Political Cooperation and the United States," *Journal of Common Market Studies*, June 1987, p. 278. Reinhardt Rummel and Wolfgang Wessels, "Federal Republic of Germany: New Responsibilities, Old Constraints," in Christopher Hill, ed., *National Foreign Policies and European Political Cooperation* (London: George Allen and Unwin, 1983), pp. 40-45; Evan Luard, "A European Foreign Policy?" *International Affairs*, Fall 1986, p. 573.
58. Simon Serfaty, "Atlantic Fantasies," in Robert W. Tucker and Linda Wrigley, eds., *The Atlantic Alliance and Its Critics* (New York: Praeger, 1983), pp. 95-128.
59. This point is developed at greater length in Simon Serfaty, *After Reagan: False Starts, Missed Opportunities & New Beginnings* (Lanham, Md.: University Press of America, 1989).

Chapter 4: Defining Europe

1. Monnet, *Memoirs*, p. 524.
2. Edward Hallett Carr, *Nationalism and After* (New York: Macmillan, 1945), pp. 36-43.
3. Quoted by Lord Roll of Ipsen, *Whither Europe in the World Economy?* The Ernest Sturc Memorial Lecture, April 11, 1985, p. 8.
4. As told by Spain's prime minister, Felipe González, in an interview with the *Financial Times*, May 9, 1991, "A better balance of rich and poor."
5. Quoted in Françoise de La Serre and Philippe Moreau Defarges, "France: A Penchant for Leadership," in Christopher Hill, ed., *National Foreign Policies and European Political Cooperation* (London: George Allen and Unwin, 1983), p. 57.
6. Harrison and Serfaty, *A Socialist France and Western Security*, pp. 9-10.
7. See Denis MacShane, *François Mitterrand: A Political Odyssey* (New York: University Books, 1983), p. 72; and Catherine Nau, *The Black and the Red* (San Diego, Calif.: Harcourt Brace Jovanovich, 1987), pp. 151-52.
8. Richard Corbett and Juliet Lodge, "Progress and Prospects," in Juliet Lodge, ed., *European Union: The European Community in Search of a Future* (New York: St. Martin's Press, 1986), p. 155.
9. According to Garrett Fitzgerald, who was Ireland's prime minister at the time: "The British Prime Minister . . . simulated surprise very successfully if she did in fact know about this procedure." "1992 and European Economic Unity," *L.S.E. Quarterly*, Autumn 1989, p. 194. See also Otto Schmuck, "The European Parliament's Draft Treaty Establishing the European Union, 1979-1984," and Richard Corbett, "The 1985 Intergovernmental Conference and the Single European Act," in Roy Pryce ed., *The Dynamics of European Union* (London: Croom Helm, 1982), p. 189 and p. 249, respectively.
10. Monnet, *Memoirs*, p. 523.
11. A.J. Marques Mendes, "The Contribution of the European Community to Economic Growth," *Journal of Common Market Studies*, June 1986, p. 272.

12.

Impact of Integration on the Growth Rate of Member Countries

Country	1961-72 Actual Growth	EEC Impact	1974-81 Actual Growth	EEC Impact
Belg/Lux	4.56	2.35	2.03	0.71
Denmark			1.98	-0.64
France	5.40	-2.71	2.66	1.57
Germany	4.39	-0.02	2.65	0.91
Holland	5.17	2.94	1.99	0.53
Ireland			3.84	0.31
Italy	4.97	1.04	2.74	0.42
UK			1.24	0.37

Source: Mendes, *The Contribution of the European Community,* pp. 266-69.

13. Stefan Wagstyl, "Japanese overseas investment in first fall since 1983," *Financial Times,* June 4, 1991, and "EC attracts more investment than US," *Financial Times,* June 11, 1991.

14. Quoted in Jacques Fauvet, *La IVème république* (Paris: Fayard, 1959), pp. 34-35.

15. Rolf J. Langhammer and Ulrich Hiemenz, "Declining Competitiveness of EC Suppliers in ASEAN Markets: Singular Case or Symptom?" *Journal of Common Market Studies,* December 1985, pp. 105-19.

16. Carlo de Benedetti, "Europe's New Role in a Global Market," in Andrew J. Pierre, ed., *A High Technology Gap? Europe, America and Japan* (New York: Council on Foreign Relations, 1987), p. 77.

17. Commission of the European Community, *A Frontier-Free Europe* (Brussels, 1988), pp. 16-17. Norman S. Fieleke, "Europe in 1992," *New England Economic Review,* Federal Reserve Bank of Boston, May/June 1989, p. 14.

18. "Italy Cannot Compete," *The International Economy,* July-August 1989, p. 77. Also, Clemente Signoroni, "Strategies for a European Corporation," *European Affairs,* Winter 1987, pp. 90-94.

19. See, for example, Henry Kissinger's account of the "inevitable" linkage between security and economic issues in *Years of Upheaval,* pp. 902-16.

20. David Henderson, *1992: The External Dimension,* The Group of Thirty, Occasional Papers, No. 25 (1989), p. 14.

21. Remarks at the Columbia Institute, Conference on 1992, Washington, D.C., February 24, 1989; "U.S.-EC Cooperation Increases As the Single Market Takes Shape," *Business America,* January 15, 1990, p. 2.

22. Hubert Curien, "The Revival of Europe," in Andrew J. Pierre, ed., *A High Technology Gap? Europe, America, and Japan,* p. 46.

23. John Peterson, "Technology Policy in Europe: Explaining the Framework Programme and Eureka in Theory and Practice," *Journal of Common Market Studies,* March 1991, pp. 269-70; Stanley Woods, *Western Europe: Technology and the Future,* Atlantic Papers (London: Croom Helm, 1987), pp. 82-92.

24. De Benedetti, "Europe's New Role in a Global Market," p. 73.

25. Robert Van Tulden, ed., *European Multinationals in Core Technologies* (Geneva: John Wiley & Sons, 1988), pp. 40-44.

26. Alan Crane, "Only the nimblest will survive," *Financial Times*, April 28, 1991. Guy de Jonquieres, "Limited scope in cross-border mergers," *Financial Times*, September 24, 1990.
27. William Dawkins and John Wyles, "Logical link-up of European giants," *Financial Times*, October 5, 1990.
28. Mike Hobday, "The European Semiconductor Industry: Resurgence and Rationalization," *Journal of Common Market Studies*, December 1989, p. 164.
29. Charles Leadbeater, "A Marriage of Convenience," *Financial Times*, July 3, 1990.
30. John Peterson, "Technology Policy in Europe," p. 281.
31. Albert Bressand, "Beyond interdependence: 1992 as a global challenge," *International Affairs*, January 1990, pp. 52-53. De Benedetti, "Europe's New Role in a Global Market," p. 79.
32. See "The Lure of 1992," *Economist*, November 18, 1989.
33. Hugh Seton-Watson, *The East European Revolution* (New York: Praeger, 1951), pp. 46-47.
34. "Walesa warns that Poland faces threat of civil war," *Financial Times*, November 30, 1990.

Chapter 5: Taking Europe Seriously

1. Arthur H. Vandenberg, Jr., ed., *The Private Papers of Senator Vandenberg* (Boston: Houghton Mifflin, 1952), p. 10.
2. Richard J. Walton, *Henry Wallace, Harry Truman, and the Cold War* (New York: Viking Press, 1976), p. 127.
3. Daniel Yergin, *Shattered Peace: The Origins of the Cold War and the National Security State* (Boston: Houghton Mifflin, 1977), p. 247.
4. See, for example, *Life*'s special issue on the Soviet Union, March 29, 1943.
5. Kennan, *Memoirs, 1925-1950*, pp. 240-42.
6. Truman, *Memoirs*, vol. 1, p. 97.
7. Vandenberg, *The Private Papers of Senator Vandenberg*, p. 165.
8. "American Myth and Legend," *New York Herald Tribune*, January 14, 1946. Joseph G. Goulden, *The Best Years, 1945-1950* (New York: Atheneum, 1976), p. 215.
9. Dean Acheson, *Present at the Creation*, p. 365.
10. Richard P. Stebbins, *The U.S. in World Affairs, 1953* (New York: Harper & Row, 1955), pp. 18-22.
11. Kennan, *Memoirs, 1925-1950*, p. 367.
12. Lawrence S. Kaplan, ed., *NATO and the Policy of Containment* (Lexington, Mass.: D.C. Heath, 1962), p. 21.
13. Dean Acheson, Radio Address of March 18, 1949, *Department of State Bulletin*, vol. XX, p. 387.
14. Vandenberg, *The Private Papers of Senator Vandenberg*, pp. 419, 495.
15. Warner, "Britain and Europe in 1948," p. 29.
16. Robert E. Osgood, *NATO, The Entangling Alliance* (Chicago: Chicago University Press, 1962), p. 50.
17. McGeorge Bundy, ed., *The Pattern of Responsibility* (Boston: Houghton Mifflin, 1951), p. 77. Also, Paul H. Nitze, "America: An Honest Broker," *Foreign Affairs*, Fall 1990, pp. 4-5.
18. Quoted in Warner, "Britain and Europe in 1948," p. 32.
19. Selig Adler, *The Isolationist Impulse* (New York: Macmillan, 1957), p. 14.
20. De Gaulle, *Mémoires d'espoir*, p. 231.
21. Monnet, *Memoirs*, p. 272.
22. Vandenberg, *The Private Papers of Senator Vandenberg*, pp. 488-91.

23. Bruce Bernard, "American Business is Bullish on Europe," *Europe*, September 1990, pp. 6-8.
24. David Gardner, "Southern discomfort," *Financial Times*, June 18, 1991.
25. David Buchan, "EC's cash mountain causes a quarrel," *Financial Times*, October 27, 1989.

Chapter 6: Imagining Europe After the Cold War
1. Monnet, *Memoirs*, pp. 523-24.
2. See W.O. Henderson, *The Zollverein* (London: Frank Cass, 1968), pp. 246-62.
3. Carl J. Friedrich, *Europe: An Emergent Nation?* (New York: Harper & Row, 1969), p. 196.
4. Quoted in Kieran Cooke, "The piper calls the tune," *Financial Times*, April 25, 1991.
5. Quoted by Edward Mortimer, "Balancing the Democratic Deficit," *Financial Times*, July 3, 1990.
6. Michael Calingaert, *The 1992 Challenge from Europe: Development of the European Community's Internal Market* (Washington, D.C.: National Planning Association, 1988), pp. 13-19. Jacques Perkmans and Peter Robson, "The Aspirations of the White Paper," *Journal of Common Market Studies*, March 1987, p. 181. John Pinder, "The Political Economy of Integration in Europe: Policies and Institutions in East and West," *Journal of Common Market Studies*, September 1986, p. 1.
7. Jean-Louis Quermone, "Existe-t-il un modèle politique européen?" *Revue Française de Science Politique*, April 1990, pp. 192-210.
8. Robert E. Hunter, "Future European Security," *Washington Quarterly*, Autumn 1990, p. 56.
9. Andrew Shonfield, *Europe: Journey to an Unknown Destination* (Baltimore, Md.: Penguin Books, 1973), p. 9.
10. Quoted in Kenneth N. Waltz, *Man, the State, and War* (New York: Columbia University Press, 1959), pp. 183-84.

Index

About the Author

Simon Serfaty is research professor of U.S. foreign policy at the Paul H. Nitze School of Advanced International Studies of the Johns Hopkins University in Washington, D.C. He is a graduate of Hunter College in New York, New York, and received his M.A. and Ph.D. from the Johns Hopkins University in 1964-67.

Professor Serfaty has been at the School of Advanced International Studies since 1972, following a four-year stay in the department of political science at the University of California in Los Angeles. He served as director of the Johns Hopkins Center of European Studies in Bologna, Italy, in 1972-76, director of the Washington Center of Foreign Policy Research in 1978-80, and executive director of the Johns Hopkins Foreign Policy Institute in 1984-91. He has lectured widely in the United States and in about forty different countries around the world on American foreign policy generally and on specific issues involving transatlantic and intra-European relations among others.

He is the author of *France, de Gaulle, & Europe: The Policy of the Fourth and Fifth Republics Toward the Continent* (1968), *The Elusive Enemy: American Foreign Policy Since World War II* (1972), *Fading Partnership: America and Europe After 30 Years* (1979), *The United States, Europe and the Third World: Allies and Adversaries* (1980), *A Socialist France and Western Security* (with Michael M. Harrison, 1981), *American Foreign Policy in a Hostile World: Dangerous Years* (1984), *Les années difficiles: La politique étrangère des Etats-Unis de Truman à Reagan* (1986), and *After Reagan: False Starts, Missed Opportunities & New Beginnings* (1989).